SO-BLK-023

Homemade Desserts

ideals

Contents

A very special thank you to the following for their cooperation and help in supplying selected recipes from their test kitchens and files:

American Butter Institute; American Dairy Association; California Fruit Exchange; California Pistachio Commission; California Strawberry Advisory Board; California Table Grape Commission; California Tree Fruit Agreement; National Cherry Growers and Industries Foundation; National Red Cherry Institute, Grand Rapids, Michigan; North Carolina Yam Commission; Northwest Purple Prune Plum Growers; Ocean Spray; Oregon Fruit Products; Oregon, Washington, and California Pear Bureaus, Pacific Bartlett Growers, Inc., Portland, Oregon; Pacific Kitchens, Seattle, Washington; Potato Chip Information Bureau; United Fresh Fruit and Vegetable Association.

Edited by Julie Hogan

Published by Ideals Publishing Corporation
11315 Watertown Plank Road
Milwaukee, Wisconsin 53226
Published simultaneously in Canada

Cover recipe:
Old-Fashioned Pound Cake, page 11.
Bake in two 9-inch round pans.
Split each layer in half; fill and
frost with Buttercream Frosting, page 5.
Garnish with fresh strawberries and
toasted almonds.

Fresh Fruit Parfait, page 41

Cakes

Chocolate Chip Date Cake

Makes 12 to 15 servings

    1 package (8 ounces) dates, chopped
    1 teaspoon baking soda
    1 cup hot water
    1 cup butter *or* margarine
    1 cup sugar
    2 eggs
 1¾ cups sifted flour
    2 teaspoons unsweetened cocoa
    1 teaspoon salt
    1 package (6 ounces) semisweet chocolate chips
    ½ cup chopped nuts
      Whipped cream, optional

Grease and flour a 13 x 9-inch baking pan; set aside. In a small bowl, combine dates, baking soda, and water; let stand until cool. Preheat oven to 350° F. In a large mixing bowl, cream butter and sugar until light and fluffy. Add eggs, one at a time, beating well after each addition. In a separate bowl, stir flour, cocoa, and salt. Alternately add dry ingredients and date mixture to creamed mixture, beating well after each addition. Spread batter in prepared pan. Sprinkle with chocolate chips and nuts. Bake for 35 to 40 minutes or until a wooden pick inserted in the center comes out clean. Cool in pan on a wire rack. Serve with whipped cream, if desired.

Chocolate Pound Cake

Makes 12 servings

    ½ cup butter *or* margarine
 1½ cups sugar
    2 eggs
    ½ cup unsweetened cocoa
    ½ cup hot coffee *or* water
    2 cups sifted flour
    1 cup buttermilk
 1½ teaspoons baking soda
    2 teaspoons vanilla

Grease a 9 x 5-inch loaf pan; set aside. Preheat oven to 350° F. In a large mixing bowl, cream butter and sugar until smooth. Add eggs, one at a time, beating well after each addition. Blend in cocoa and hot coffee. Alternately add flour and buttermilk to chocolate mixture, beating well after each addition. Stir in baking soda and vanilla; blend just until smooth. Pour batter into prepared pan. Bake for 20 to 30 minutes or until top springs back when lightly touched. Cool in pan 10 minutes before turning out onto a wire rack to cool completely.

Ginger Cake
with Orange Glazed Pears

Makes 12 to 14 servings

 2¼ cups flour
 1½ teaspoons ground ginger
    1 teaspoon baking powder
    1 teaspoon baking soda
    1 teaspoon ground cinnamon
    ½ teaspoon salt
    ½ cup packed brown sugar
    2 eggs, lightly beaten
    1 cup milk
    ½ cup molasses
    ½ cup vegetable oil
      Orange Glazed Pears (recipe follows)

Grease and flour a 10-inch tube pan; set aside. Preheat oven to 350° F. In a large mixing bowl, sift together flour, ginger, baking powder, baking soda, cinnamon, and salt. Stir in brown sugar. In a separate bowl, combine eggs, milk, molasses, and oil; blend well. Add liquids to flour mixture; blend well. Pour into prepared pan. Bake for 45 to 50 minutes or until a wooden pick inserted in the center comes out clean. Cool in pan 5 minutes before inverting onto a serving plate. Arrange Orange Glazed Pears around sides and top of cake. Spoon remaining glaze over cake.

Orange Glazed Pears

    1 can (6 ounces) frozen orange juice concentrate, thawed
    ¼ cup sugar
    1 tablespoon sherry
    2 pears, cored and sliced

In a medium saucepan, combine orange juice concentrate, sugar, and sherry; blend well. Add pears. Simmer until tender.

Pumpkin Sheet Cake

Makes 14 to 16 servings

- 1 cup vegetable oil
- 4 eggs
- 2 cups sugar
- 1 can (15 ounces) pumpkin
- 2 cups flour
- 2 teaspoons baking powder
- 1 teaspoon baking soda
- ½ teaspoon salt
- 2 teaspoons ground cinnamon
- ½ teaspoon ground ginger
- ½ teaspoon ground cloves
- ½ teaspoon ground nutmeg
- ½ cup chopped nuts
- Cream Cheese Frosting (recipe follows)

Grease a 16 x 12-inch baking pan; set aside. Preheat oven to 350° F. In a large mixing bowl, combine oil, eggs, sugar, and pumpkin; blend well. In a separate bowl, sift together flour, baking powder, baking soda, salt, and spices. Gradually blend dry ingredients into pumpkin mixture. Stir in nuts. Pour batter into prepared pan. Bake for 25 to 30 minutes or until a wooden pick inserted in the center comes out clean. Cool in pan on a wire rack. Frost with Cream Cheese Frosting. Cut into squares.

Cream Cheese Frosting

Makes frosting for one layer or sheet cake

- 2 packages (3 ounces each) cream cheese, softened
- 6 tablespoons butter *or* margarine, softened
- 1 tablespoon milk
- 1 teaspoon vanilla
- 1 box (1 pound) powdered sugar, sifted

In a small mixing bowl, combine cream cheese and butter; blend well. Beat in milk and vanilla. Gradually add powdered sugar, beating until of spreading consistency.

Carrot Cake

Makes 10 to 16 servings

- 2 cups flour
- 2 cups sugar
- 2 teaspoons baking soda
- 2 teaspoons ground cinnamon
- 1 teaspoon salt
- 4 eggs, well beaten
- 1½ cups vegetable oil
- 3 cups grated raw carrots
- Cream Cheese Frosting (above)

Grease and flour two 9-inch round baking pans; set aside. Preheat oven to 350° F. In a large mixing bowl, sift together flour, sugar, baking soda, cinnamon, and salt. Add eggs and oil; blend well. Add carrots; blend well. Pour batter into prepared pans. Bake for 40 minutes or until a wooden pick inserted in the center comes out clean. Cool in pan 10 minutes before turning out onto a wire rack to cool completely. Spread Cream Cheese Frosting between layers and on sides and top of cake.

Waldorf Astoria Cake

Makes 10 to 16 servings

- 1 cup vegetable shortening
- 1½ cups sugar
- 2 eggs
- 2 ounces red food coloring
- 2¼ cups flour
- 1 teaspoon salt
- 1 teaspoon baking soda
- 1 teaspoon vanilla
- 1 cup buttermilk
- Buttercream Frosting (recipe follows)

Grease and flour two 9-inch round baking pans; set aside. Preheat oven to 350° F. In a large mixing bowl, cream shortening and sugar until light and fluffy. Add eggs, one at a time, beating well after each addition. Blend in food coloring. In a separate bowl, sift together flour, salt, and baking soda. Alternately add dry ingredients and buttermilk to creamed mixture, beginning and ending with dry ingredients, beating well after each addition. Beat in vanilla. Pour batter into prepared pans. Bake 30 to 35 minutes or until a wooden pick inserted in the center comes out clean. Cool in pans 10 minutes before turning out onto a wire rack to cool completely. Spread frosting between layers and over sides and top of cake.

Buttercream Frosting

Makes frosting for one 2-layer cake

- 1 cup milk
- 3 tablespoons flour
- 1 cup butter *or* margarine
- 1 cup sugar
- 1 teaspoon vanilla

In a small saucepan, combine milk and flour; blend well. Cook over low heat, stirring constantly until thickened. Remove from heat; let stand until cool. Cream butter and sugar until light and fluffy. Beat in vanilla. Add milk mixture; beat until consistency of whipped cream.

Cakes

Daffodil Cake

Makes 12 to 14 servings

> 6 eggs, separated
> ¼ teaspoon salt
> 1 teaspoon cream of tartar
> 1½ cups superfine sugar
> 1 teaspoon lemon extract
> 1¼ cups sifted cake flour, divided
> 1 teaspoon vanilla
>   Powdered sugar, optional

Preheat oven to 200° F. In a large mixing bowl, beat egg whites, salt, and cream of tartar until stiff but not dry. Fold in sugar until blended. Divide egg white mixture in half. In a small mixing bowl, beat egg yolks until light-colored. To one portion of the egg white mixture, add egg yolks and lemon extract; fold gently to blend. Fold in ¾ cup flour until just blended. To the remaining egg white mixture, fold in vanilla and remaining ½ cup flour. Drop alternate tablespoonfuls of the 2 batters into an ungreased 10-inch tube pan. Place pan in oven. Increase oven temperature to 325° F. Bake for 1½ hours. Invert pan onto a funnel or soda bottle to cool. Loosen edges of cake with a spatula or knife. Invert onto a serving plate. Sift powdered sugar over the top through a lace doily, if desired.

Poppy Seed Cake

Makes 10 to 16 servings

> ½ cup poppy seed
> 1 cup milk
> 1 teaspoon vanilla
> ¾ cup butter
> 1½ cups sugar
> 2 cups sifted flour
> 2 teaspoons baking powder
> ½ teaspoon salt
> 4 egg whites
>   Custard Filling (recipe follows)
>   Buttercream Frosting (page 5)

In a small bowl, combine poppy seed, milk, and vanilla. Refrigerate overnight. Grease and flour two 8-inch round baking pans; set aside. Preheat oven to 350° F. In a mixing bowl, cream butter and sugar until smooth. In a separate bowl, sift together flour, baking powder, and salt. Alternately add dry ingredients and poppy seed mixture to creamed mixture, beginning and ending with dry ingredients, beating well after each addition. In a small mixing bowl, beat egg whites until stiff but not dry. Gently fold egg whites into batter. Pour batter into prepared pans. Bake for 30 to 35 minutes or until a wooden pick inserted in the center comes out clean. Cool in pans 5 minutes before turning out onto a wire rack to cool completely. Spread Custard Filling between layers. Spread sides and top with Buttercream Frosting.

Custard Filling

> ¾ cup sugar
> 4 egg yolks
> 2 tablespoons cornstarch
> 1½ cups milk
> ¼ teaspoon salt
> 1 teaspoon vanilla
> ½ cup chopped nuts

In the top of a double boiler, combine sugar, egg yolks, cornstarch, milk, and salt. Cook over boiling water, stirring constantly, about 5 minutes or until thickened. Remove from heat; let stand until cool. Stir in vanilla and nuts.

Cranberry Swirl Cake

Makes 12 to 14 servings

> ½ cup butter or margarine
> 1 cup sugar
> 2 eggs
> 2 cups flour
> 1 teaspoon baking powder
> 1 teaspoon baking soda
> ½ teaspoon salt
> 1 cup dairy sour cream
> 1 teaspoon almond extract
> 1 can (8 ounces) whole berry cranberry sauce
> ½ cup chopped nuts

Grease and flour a 10-inch tube pan; set aside. Preheat oven to 350° F. In a mixing bowl, cream butter and sugar until smooth. Add eggs, one at a time, beating well after each addition. In a separate bowl, sift together flour, baking powder, baking soda, and salt. Alternately add dry ingredients and sour cream to creamed mixture, beating well after each addition. Beat in almond extract. Pour half of batter into prepared pan. Spoon cranberry sauce on top of batter. Spoon remaining batter over cranberries. Sprinkle with nuts. Bake for 50 to 55 minutes or until golden. Cool in pan 5 minutes before turning out onto a wire rack to cool completely.

Old-Fashioned Pound Cake, 11, with Lemon Glaze, 8

Cakes

Spumoni Chiffon Cake

Makes 10 servings

> 2 eggs, separated
> 1½ cups sugar, divided
> 1¾ cups sifted flour
> ¾ teaspoon baking soda
> 1 teaspoon salt
> ⅓ cup vegetable oil
> 1 cup buttermilk, divided
> 2 squares (1 ounce each) unsweetened baking chocolate, melted
> Green Pistachio Filling (recipe follows)
> Pink Peppermint Filling (recipe follows)
> Gold Rum Filling (recipe follows)
> Spicy Cocoa Topping (recipe follows)
> 2 pints whipping cream
> 1 cup powdered sugar

Grease and flour two 9-inch round baking pans; set aside. Preheat oven to 350° F. In a small mixing bowl, beat egg whites until foamy. Gradually beat in ½ cup of the sugar, beating until stiff and glossy; set aside. In a large mixing bowl, sift together flour, remaining 1 cup sugar, baking soda, and salt. Add oil and ½ cup milk; beat 1 minute on medium speed, scraping sides and bottom of bowl often. Blend in remaining ½ cup milk, egg yolks, and melted chocolate; beat 1 minute. Gently fold in egg whites until no streaks of white remain. Pour batter into prepared pans. Bake for 25 to 30 minutes or until golden. Cool in pans 10 minutes before turning out onto a wire rack to cool completely. In a large mixing bowl, gradually add powdered sugar to whipping cream, beating until soft peaks form. Prepare fillings and topping. Fill layers with Green Pistachio, Pink Peppermint, and Golden Rum Fillings, in that order. Spread Spicy Cocoa Topping on sides and top of cake. Chill well before serving. (Cake can also be frozen. Thaw 2 to 3 hours before serving.)

Green Pistachio Filling

> 4 to 6 drops green food coloring
> 1 teaspoon vanilla
> ¼ cup chopped pistachio nuts

To ⅕ of the whipped cream, fold in food coloring, vanilla, and nuts.

Pink Peppermint Filling

> 4 to 6 drops red food coloring
> ¼ cup crushed peppermint candies

To ⅕ of the whipped cream, fold in food coloring and crushed candies.

Gold Rum Filling

> 4 to 6 drops yellow food coloring
> 1 teaspoon rum flavoring

To ⅕ of the whipped cream, fold in food coloring and rum flavoring.

Spicy Cocoa Topping

> ½ teaspoon ground cinnamon
> 3 tablespoons sifted unsweetened cocoa

To remaining ⅖ whipped cream, fold in cinnamon and cocoa.

Carrot Mincemeat Cake

Makes 12 to 14 servings

> 1 package (9 ounces) mincemeat, crumbled
> 2 cups grated carrots
> ½ cup chopped nuts
> 2 cups flour, divided
> 1 cup packed brown sugar
> ¾ cup vegetable oil
> ¼ cup lemon juice
> 3 eggs
> 2 teaspoons baking powder
> 1 teaspoon baking soda
> 1 teaspoon salt
> Lemon Glaze (recipe follows)

Grease and flour a 10-inch fluted tube pan; set aside. Preheat oven to 325° F. Combine mincemeat, carrots, nuts, and ½ cup flour; toss lightly to mix; set aside. In a large mixing bowl, combine brown sugar, oil, and lemon juice; blend well. Add eggs, one at a time, beating well after each addition. In a separate bowl, combine remaining 1½ cups flour, baking powder, baking soda, and salt. Gradually add sifted ingredients to egg mixture; beat until smooth. Stir in mincemeat mixture; blend well. Pour batter into prepared pan. Bake for 1 hour or until a wooden pick inserted near the center comes out clean. Cool in pan 15 minutes before turning out of pan to cool completely. Drizzle with Lemon Glaze.

Lemon Glaze

> 2 tablespoons butter or margarine
> 4 teaspoons lemon juice
> 1 cup sifted powdered sugar

In a small saucepan, combine butter and lemon juice; cook, stirring constantly until butter melts. Add powdered sugar; stir until smooth.

Angel Food Cake with Strawberry Icing

Makes 12 to 14 servings

  1 cup sifted cake flour
1½ cups sugar, divided
 13 egg whites, room temperature
  2 teaspoons cream of tartar
  ¼ teaspoon salt
1½ teaspoons vanilla
  ½ teaspoon almond extract
    Strawberry Icing (recipe follows)

Preheat oven to 350° F. Sift together flour and ½ cup of the sugar 3 times; set aside. In a large mixing bowl, beat egg whites, cream of tartar, and salt until foamy. Add remaining 1 cup sugar, one tablespoon at a time, beating at high speed until stiff peaks form. Stir in vanilla and almond extracts. Gradually and gently fold in flour mixture. Carefully spoon batter into an ungreased 10-inch tube pan. Draw a metal knife through the batter a few times to break up air bubbles. Bake for 35 minutes or until golden. Invert pan onto a funnel or soda bottle to cool. Loosen edges of cake with a spatula or knife. Gently transfer from pan to a serving plate. Frost with Strawberry Icing. Chill 2 to 3 hours before serving. Store cake in the refrigerator.

Strawberry Icing

Makes frosting for 1 angel food cake

  1 cup whole strawberries, slightly crushed
  1 cup granulated sugar
  2 egg whites
  ⅛ teaspoon salt

In a medium mixing bowl, combine strawberries and sugar. Beat until berries are mashed. Add egg whites and salt. Beat on high speed until stiff peaks form.

Toasted Butter Pecan Cake

Makes 12 servings

  2 cups chopped pecans, divided
1¼ cups butter, divided
  3 cups sifted flour
  2 teaspoons baking powder
  ½ teaspoon salt
  2 cups sugar
  4 eggs
  1 cup milk
  2 teaspoons vanilla
    Powdered Sugar Frosting (recipe follows)

Grease and flour three 8- or 9-inch round baking pans; set aside. Preheat oven to 350° F. Melt ¼ cup butter on a baking sheet. Add pecans; toast in oven 20 to 25 minutes, stirring frequently, until golden. Sift together flour, baking powder, and salt; set aside. In a large mixing bowl, cream remaining 1 cup butter and sugar until light and fluffy. Add eggs, one at a time, beating well after each addition. Alternately add flour mixture and milk, beginning and ending with flour, beating well after each addition. Stir in vanilla and 1⅓ cups of the pecans. (Reserve ⅔ cup pecans for frosting.) Pour batter into prepared pans. Bake 20 minutes or until a wooden pick inserted in the center comes out clean. Cool in pans 10 minutes before turning out onto a wire rack to cool completely. Spread frosting between layers and over sides and top of cake.

Powdered Sugar Frosting

Makes frosting for one 3-layer cake

  ¼ cup butter *or* margarine
  1 box (1 pound) powdered sugar, sifted
  4 to 6 tablespoons evaporated milk *or* half-and-half
  1 teaspoon vanilla
    Reserved ⅔ cup toasted pecans

In a medium mixing bowl, cream butter until light and fluffy. Gradually beat in powdered sugar and milk until of spreading consistency. Beat in vanilla. Stir in pecans.

Breath of Spring Cake

Makes 12 servings

  ½ cup vegetable shortening
1⅓ cups sugar
  1 teaspoon salt
  2 cups flour
  1 cup milk, divided
  1 tablespoon baking powder
  2 eggs

Grease a 13 x 9-inch baking pan; set aside. Preheat oven to 375° F. In a large mixing bowl, cream shortening, sugar, and salt. Alternately add flour and ⅔ cup milk, beginning and ending with flour, beating well after each addition. Add baking powder; blend well. Add eggs, remaining ⅓ cup milk, and vanilla; blend well. Beat 2 minutes on medium speed or until batter is thin and smooth. Pour batter into prepared pan. Bake for 25 minutes or until a wooden pick inserted in the center comes out clean. Cool in pan on a wire rack. Frost if desired.

Devil's Food Cake
with Mint Seven-Minute Frosting
Makes 10 to 16 servings

 ¾ cup boiling water
 3 squares (1 ounce each) unsweetened baking
  chocolate
2¼ cups sifted cake flour
1½ teaspoons baking soda
 ¾ teaspoon baking powder
 ¾ teaspoon salt
 ¾ cup vegetable shortening
1⅞ cups packed brown sugar
 3 eggs, well beaten
1½ teaspoons vanilla
 ¾ cup sour milk*
  Mint Seven-Minute Frosting (recipe follows)

Grease and flour two 9-inch round baking pans; set aside. Preheat oven to 350° F. In a small saucepan, pour boiling water over chocolate; stir over low heat until thick and smooth; cool. Sift together flour, baking soda, baking powder, and salt; set aside. In a large mixing bowl, cream shortening and sugar until smooth. Add eggs and vanilla; blend well. Stir in cooled chocolate. Alternately add dry ingredients and milk to creamed mixture, blending well after each addition. Pour batter into prepared pans. Bake for 30 minutes or until a wooden pick inserted in the center comes out clean. Cool in pans 10 minutes before turning out onto a wire rack to cool completely. Spread frosting between layers and over top and sides of cake.

*To sour milk, use 1 tablespoon vinegar plus milk to equal ¾ cup.

Mint Seven-Minute Frosting

Makes frosting for 9-inch layer cake

1½ cups sugar
⅓ cup water
 2 egg whites
1½ teaspoons light corn syrup
 ¼ teaspoon salt
 1 teaspoon vanilla
 ½ cup crushed after-dinner mints
  Green food coloring

In the top of a double boiler, combine sugar, water, egg whites, corn syrup, and salt. Beat with a rotary beater until well blended. Place over rapidly boiling water; beat 7 to 10 minutes or until stiff peaks form. Remove from heat. Stir in vanilla, mints, and food coloring to tint frosting a light green. Beat until frosting is of spreading consistency.

Chocolate Potato Cake
Makes 12 to 15 servings

 1 cup butter *or* margarine, softened
 2 cups sugar
 4 eggs, separated
 1 cup shaved semisweet chocolate
 1 cup unseasoned leftover mashed potatoes
 ½ cup chopped walnuts
1½ cups flour
 1 teaspoon ground cinnamon
 2 teaspoons baking powder
 ½ teaspoon salt
 ½ cup half-and-half *or* milk

Grease and flour a 13 x 9-inch baking pan; set aside. Preheat oven to 350° F. In a large mixing bowl, cream butter and sugar until light and fluffy. Add egg yolks, one at a time, beating well after each addition. Add shaved chocolate and mashed potatoes; blend until smooth. Stir in nuts. In a separate bowl, sift together flour, cinnamon, baking powder, and salt. Alternately add dry ingredients and half-and-half to creamed mixture, beating well after each addition. In a small bowl, beat egg whites and salt until stiff but not dry. Carefully fold egg whites into batter. Pour batter into prepared pan. Bake for 50 to 60 minutes or until a wooden pick inserted in the center comes out clean. Sprinkle with powdered sugar, if desired. Cool in pan on a wire rack.

Note: Cake can also be baked in a 10-inch tube or Bundt pan.

Old-Fashioned Pound Cake

Makes 12 to 14 servings

 1 pound butter (2 cups)
 1 pound sugar (3½ cups)
 1 pound eggs (10 large or 12 small)
 1 pound sifted flour (4 cups)
 1 teaspoon vanilla
  Lemon Medley or Any-Berry Topping,
  (page 37), optional

Grease a 10-inch tube pan; set aside. Preheat oven to 300° F. In a large mixing bowl, cream butter and sugar until light and fluffy. Add eggs, one at a time, beating well after each addition. Gradually add flour; blend well. Pour batter into prepared pan. Bake 2 hours or until a wooden pick inserted near the center comes out clean. Cool in pan 10 minutes before turning out onto a wire rack to cool completely. Serve with lemon or berry topping, if desired.

Crisps, Kuchens, and Upside-Down Cakes

Pear Coconut Crisp

Makes 6 to 8 servings

  6 fresh pears, cored, peeled, and sliced
  1 cup packed brown sugar, divided
  1 teaspoon grated orange peel
  ½ teaspoon ground cinnamon
  ½ teaspoon ground nutmeg
  ½ cup flour, divided
  ¼ cup orange juice
  ¼ cup butter or margarine
  1 cup flaked coconut
    Whipping cream or half-and-half, optional

Preheat oven to 350° F. In a bowl, combine pears, ½ cup brown sugar, orange peel, cinnamon, nutmeg, and 2 tablespoons flour; toss lightly to mix. Place pear mixture in a shallow 2-quart casserole. Pour orange juice over pears. In a small bowl, combine remaining brown sugar and flour. Cut in butter with a pastry blender or two knives until crumbly. Stir in coconut. Sprinkle crumb mixture over pears. Cover and bake 40 minutes. Uncover; bake 10 to 20 minutes or until pears are tender. Serve warm with cream, if desired.

Pear Lunch Cake

Makes 6 to 8 servings

  3 fresh pears
  2 cups sifted flour
  2 teaspoons baking soda
  1 teaspoon salt
  1 teaspoon cinnamon
  ½ teaspoon ground nutmeg
  ½ teaspoon ground ginger
  1½ cups packed brown sugar, divided
  2 eggs
  ½ cup butter or margarine, melted
  2 tablespoons lemon juice
  ½ cup chopped pecans, divided

Grease a 9-inch square baking dish; set aside. Preheat oven to 350° F. Halve, core, and chop 2 pears to measure 1½ cups. Reserve remaining pear for topping. In a large bowl, mix flour, baking soda, salt, spices, and 1 cup plus 6 tablespoons brown sugar. Stir in chopped pears, eggs, butter, lemon juice, and 6 tablespoons pecans. Beat on medium speed for 2 minutes. Pour into prepared pan. Sprinkle with remaining brown sugar and nuts. Slice remaining pear; arrange slices over nuts. Bake 30 to 40 minutes or until golden.

Perfect Peach Crisp

Makes 6 servings

  3 cups sliced fresh or drained canned peaches
  1 tablespoon lemon juice
  1 cup flour
  1 cup sugar
  ½ teaspoon salt
  1 egg, lightly beaten
  6 tablespoons butter or margarine, melted
    Ice cream, optional

Preheat oven to 375° F. Arrange peach slices in a 10 x 6-inch baking dish. Sprinkle with lemon juice. (Omit lemon juice if using canned peaches.) In a large mixing bowl, sift together flour, sugar, and salt. Add egg; toss lightly with fork until crumbly. Sprinkle crumb mixture over peaches. Drizzle melted butter over top. Bake for 35 to 40 minutes or until topping is golden. Serve with ice cream, if desired.

Cranberry Apple Crisp

Makes 9 servings

  5 cups cored, peeled, and sliced tart cooking apples
  1½ cups fresh or thawed frozen whole cranberries
  ⅓ cup granulated sugar
  ½ cup flour
  ½ cup packed brown sugar
  1 teaspoon ground cinnamon
  ¼ cup butter or margarine

Grease a 9-inch square baking pan. Preheat oven to 375° F. Layer apples and cranberries in prepared pan, sprinkling granulated sugar between layers. In a small bowl, combine flour, brown sugar, and cinnamon. Cut in butter with a pastry blender or two knives until the mixture resembles coarse crumbs. Sprinkle crumb mixture evenly over apples and cranberries. Bake for 45 minutes or until apples are tender.

Apple Kuchen

Makes 12 servings

   2 cups flour
   1 tablespoon baking powder
   ¼ teaspoon salt
   2 cups sugar, divided
   3 tablespoons vegetable shortening
   1 egg
      Milk
   7 tart cooking apples, peeled and sliced
   2 tablespoons flour
   ¾ teaspoon ground cinnamon
   2 tablespoons butter *or* margarine

Grease a 13 x 9-inch baking pan; set aside. Preheat oven to 350° F. In a large mixing bowl, combine flour, baking powder, salt, and ½ cup sugar. Cut in shortening with a pastry blender or two knives until mixture resembles coarse crumbs. In a measuring cup, combine egg and enough milk to equal 1 cup. Add to flour mixture; blend well. Press batter into prepared pan. Arrange apple slices over crust. In a small bowl, mix remaining 1½ cups sugar, 2 tablespoons flour, and cinnamon. Cut in butter until consistency of coarse crumbs. Sprinkle crumb mixture over apples. Bake for 45 to 60 minutes or until apples are tender and topping is golden.

Chocolate Upside-Down Cake

Makes 6 to 8 servings

   1 cup flour
   1¼ cups sugar, divided
   4 tablespoons unsweetened cocoa, divided
   2 teaspoons baking powder
   ¼ teaspoon salt
   ½ cup milk
   3 tablespoons butter *or* margarine, melted
   1 teaspoon vanilla
   ½ cup chopped pecans
   ½ cup packed brown sugar
   1 cup cold water

Preheat oven to 350° F. In a large mixing bowl, combine flour, ¾ cup sugar, 2 tablespoons cocoa, baking powder, and salt. Stir in milk, butter, vanilla, and pecans. Pour batter into a 10 x 8-inch baking pan. In a small bowl, combine remaining ½ cup granulated sugar, ½ cup brown sugar, and remaining 2 tablespoons cocoa. Sprinkle over batter. Carefully pour water over top. Bake 35 to 40 minutes or until set. Cut into squares and turn upside down onto serving plates.

Fruit Cocktail Cake

Makes 12 servings

   1½ cups flour
   2 tablespoons butter *or* margarine, divided
   1 cup sugar
   ¾ teaspoon salt
   1 teaspoon baking soda
   1 teaspoon vanilla
   ½ teaspoon almond extract
   1 egg, lightly beaten
   1 can (17 ounces) fruit cocktail, undrained
   1 cup chopped pecans, divided
   ¾ cup packed brown sugar
   1 tablespoon flour

Grease and flour a 9-inch square baking pan; set aside. Preheat oven to 350° F. In a large mixing bowl, combine flour, 1 tablespoon butter, sugar, salt, baking soda, vanilla, almond extract, and egg; blend well. Stir in fruit cocktail and liquid. Sprinkle ½ cup nuts in bottom of prepared pan. Pour batter over nuts. In a small bowl, mix ½ cup nuts, 1 tablespoon butter, and 1 tablespoon flour until crumbly. Sprinkle crumb mixture over batter. Bake for 40 minutes or until topping is golden.

Cranberry Pear Crisp

Makes 6 to 8 servings

   2 cups fresh *or* thawed frozen whole cranberries
   2 cups cored, peeled, and diced pears
   1 cup sugar
   ¼ cup orange juice
   ½ teaspoon ground cinnamon
   ¼ teaspoon ground mace
   ¼ cup packed brown sugar
   3 tablespoons flour
   1 teaspoon grated orange peel
   ¼ cup butter *or* margarine
   ¾ cup rolled oats
   ¾ cup chopped walnuts
      Cream *or* ice cream, optional

Preheat oven to 350° F. Butter a 1½-quart casserole. In prepared casserole, combine cranberries, pears, sugar, orange juice, cinnamon, and mace; mix well. In a medium bowl, mix brown sugar, flour, and orange peel. Cut in butter with a pastry blender or two knives until mixture resembles coarse crumbs. Stir in oats and nuts. Sprinkle crumb mixture over cranberries. Bake for 50 minutes or until golden. Serve warm or cold. Top with cream or ice cream, if desired.

Pies and Pastries

Single Piecrust

Makes crust for one 8- or 9-inch pie

- 1 cup flour
- ½ teaspoon salt
- ⅓ cup plus 1 tablespoon vegetable shortening
- 2 to 3 tablespoons cold water

In a medium bowl, combine flour and salt. Cut in shortening with a pastry blender or two knives until particles are the size of small peas. Sprinkle water, one tablespoon at a time, over flour mixture, tossing lightly with a fork to mix. Dough should hold together without being sticky. Gather dough into a ball. Roll out dough on a lightly floured surface 1 inch larger than inverted pie plate. Fit crust into pie plate. Trim and flute edge.

For Baked Piecrust:

Preheat oven to 475° F. Prick bottom of crust with a fork. Bake 8 to 10 minutes or until golden. Cool before filling.

Double Piecrust

Makes crust for one 8- or 9-inch two-crust pie

- 2 cups flour
- 1 teaspoon salt
- ⅔ cup plus 2 tablespoons vegetable shortening
- 4 to 5 tablespoons cold water

In a medium bowl, combine flour and salt. Cut in shortening with a pastry blender or two knives until particles are the size of small peas. Sprinkle water over flour mixture, one tablespoon at a time, tossing lightly with a fork to mix. Dough should hold together without being sticky. Gather dough into a ball. Divide dough in half. Roll out one half of dough on a lightly floured surface 1 inch larger than inverted pie plate. Fit crust into pie plate. Roll out remaining dough. Fill crust as recipe directs. Top with remaining crust. Press edges together to seal. Trim and flute edge. Cut slits in top to vent steam. Bake as recipe directs.

Sweet Potato Pie

Makes 6 to 8 servings

- ¼ cup butter *or* margarine, softened
- ⅔ cup packed dark brown sugar
- 4 eggs
- ¾ cup dark corn syrup
- 1 teaspoon vanilla
- 1 cup mashed cooked yams
- 1 cup chopped pecans
- 1 unbaked 9-inch Single Piecrust (page 15)
  Whole pecans
  Whipped cream, optional

Preheat oven to 400° F. In a large mixing bowl, cream butter and brown sugar until smooth. Add eggs, one at a time, beating well after each addition. Blend in corn syrup, vanilla, and yams. Stir in chopped pecans; set aside. Turn yam mixture into piecrust. Bake for 10 minutes. Reduce oven temperature to 350° F. Bake 30 minutes or until filling is set and crust is lightly browned. Cool on a wire rack. Garnish with whole pecans. Serve with whipped cream, if desired.

California Walnut Pie

Makes 6 to 8 servings

- ½ cup packed brown sugar
- 2 tablespoons flour
- 1½ cups light corn syrup
- 3 tablespoons butter *or* margarine
- ¼ teaspoon salt
- 3 eggs
- 1½ teaspoons vanilla
- 1 unbaked 9-inch single piecrust (page 15)
- 1 cup walnut halves

Preheat oven to 375° F. In a saucepan, combine brown sugar, flour, corn syrup, butter, and salt. Cook over low heat, stirring constantly, just until butter melts. In a medium mixing bowl, beat eggs and vanilla until light-colored. Add sugar mixture; blend well. Pour into piecrust. Sprinkle with walnuts. Bake on lowest shelf of oven for 40 minutes or until filling is set. Cool on a wire rack.

Black Russian Pie

Makes 6 to 8 servings

    Butter Crust (recipe follows)
 ⅓ cup coffee-flavored liqueur
 2 envelopes unflavored gelatin
 ½ cup milk
 2 eggs
 ½ cup sugar
 ⅔ cup vodka
 1½ cups whipping cream
    Chocolate curls, optional

Prepare Butter Crust; let stand until cool. Pour coffee liqueur into a blender or food processor. Add gelatin; let stand 5 minutes. In a small saucepan, heat milk to boiling; pour over gelatin mixture. Blend until gelatin dissolves. Add eggs, sugar, and vodka; blend until smooth. Cool until mixture begins to thicken. In a large mixing bowl, beat whipping cream until stiff peaks form. Fold whipped cream into gelatin mixture. Chill until mixture mounds slightly. Pour into prepared piecrust. Chill until firm, about 4 hours. Garnish with chocolate curls, if desired.

Butter Crust

Makes one 9-inch crust

 ½ cup butter, softened
 2 tablespoons sugar
 1 cup flour

In a mixing bowl, combine butter and sugar; blend well. Add flour; mix on low speed just until dough holds together. Press dough into a 9-inch pie plate. Bake at 375° F. 12 to 15 minutes or until light golden brown.

Stars and Stripes Apple Pie

Makes 6 to 8 servings

 1 unbaked 9-inch Single Piecrust (page 15)
 6 cups peeled and sliced tart apples
 ¾ cup sugar
 2½ tablespoons cornstarch
 1 tablespoon lemon juice
 1 teaspoon ground cinnamon
 ¼ cup flour
 ¼ cup packed brown sugar
 1 cup shredded Cheddar cheese
 ¾ cup crushed potato chips
    Cinnamon ice cream, optional

Preheat oven to 400° F. Combine apples, sugar, cornstarch, lemon juice, and cinnamon; toss lightly to mix; set aside. In a separate bowl, combine flour, brown sugar, cheese, and chips; blend with pastry blender until mixture resembles coarse crumbs. Turn apple mixture into piecrust. Sprinkle evenly with crumb mixture. Bake for 40 to 50 minutes or until apples are tender. If topping is browning too rapidly, cover lightly with aluminum foil. Cool on a wire rack until warm. Serve with ice cream, if desired.

Deep-Dish Pumpkin Apple Pie

Makes 6 to 8 servings

 1 unbaked 9-inch single piecrust (page 15)
    Apple Filling (recipe follows)
    Pumpkin Filling (recipe follows)

Prepare piecrust. Fit into a 9-inch deep-dish pie plate.* Prepare Apple Filling. Spread hot apple mixture evenly in crust. Prepare Pumpkin Filling. Carefully pour pumpkin mixture over apples. Preheat oven to 375° F. Bake 40 to 50 minutes or until pumpkin mixture is just set. Cool on a wire rack before serving.

*If you do not have a deep-dish pie plate, crimp edges high in the pie plate you are using and place a sheet of aluminum foil beneath pie to catch overflow.

Apple Filling

 ½ cup packed brown sugar
 1 tablespoon cornstarch
 1 teaspoon ground cinnamon
 ¼ teaspoon salt
 ½ cup water
 2 tablespoons butter *or* margarine
 4 tart cooking apples, peeled, cored, and sliced
 1 tablespoon lemon juice

In a medium saucepan, combine brown sugar, cornstarch, cinnamon, salt, water, and butter. Bring to a boil over medium heat, stirring constantly. Add apples. Cover and cook 5 to 6 minutes, stirring occasionally, until tender-crisp. Do not overcook. Stir in lemon juice.

Pumpkin Filling

 1 egg, well beaten
 1 cup canned pumpkin
 ½ cup sugar
 ¼ teaspoon salt
 ½ teaspoon ground cinnamon
 ½ teaspoon ground ginger
 ⅛ teaspoon ground cloves
 1 can (5.5 ounces) evaporated milk

In a medium bowl, blend egg, pumpkin, sugar, salt, and spices. Add milk; blend well.

Fresh Orange Tart

Makes 8 servings

    Sweet Pastry (recipe follows)
½ cup red currant jelly
4 oranges, peeled and sectioned

Prepare Sweet Pastry. In a small saucepan, melt jelly over low heat; cool slightly. Brush bottom of cooled pastry shell lightly with melted jelly. Arrange orange sections in pastry shell. Brush with remaining jelly.

Sweet Pastry

Makes one 9-inch tart shell

    2 cups flour
½ cup sugar
¼ teaspoon salt
2 egg yolks
1 teaspoon grated lemon peel
¾ cup butter *or* margarine

In a medium bowl, sift together flour, sugar, and salt. Stir in egg yolks and lemon peel with a fork. Use fingers to blend in butter until mixture holds together. Gather into a ball. Wrap in waxed paper or plastic wrap. Chill 30 minutes or until firm. Roll out dough on a lightly floured surface to a 12-inch circle. (Pastry will be fairly thick.) Fit dough into a 9-inch fluted tart pan with a removable bottom. Prick well with a fork. Line pastry shell with foil; fill with dried beans or rice. Bake at 400° F. for 6 minutes. Remove foil and beans. Bake 6 to 7 minutes or until pastry is lightly browned. Cool on a wire rack. Gently remove from pan and place on a serving plate.

Peach Chantilly Pie

Makes 6 to 8 servings

    3 to 4 fresh peaches
1½ tablespoons lemon juice
1 envelope plus 1 teaspoon unflavored gelatin
½ cup sugar
2 tablespoons orange-flavored liqueur
⅛ teaspoon salt
1 cup whipping cream
1 baked 9-inch Single Piecrust (page 15)
    Whipped cream
    Peach slices

Peel, halve, and dice peaches to measure 2¾ cups. In a blender or food processor, puree peaches to measure 2 cups. In a small saucepan, combine ½ cup peach puree with lemon juice. Sprinkle gelatin over puree; let stand 5 min-

utes to soften gelatin. Place saucepan in larger pan filled with hot water. Heat, stirring constantly, until gelatin dissolves. Stir in remaining peach puree, sugar, liqueur, and salt. Cool until mixture begins to thicken. In a small mixing bowl, beat whipping cream until stiff peaks form. Fold whipped cream into gelatin mixture. Chill until mixture mounds slightly. Pour into piecrust. Chill until firm, about 4 hours. Garnish with whipped cream and sliced peaches.

Pear Tart

Makes 6 to 8 servings

    Cinnamon Tart Shell (recipe follows)
½ teaspoon ground cinnamon
3 teaspoons sugar, divided
3 to 4 fresh Bartlett pears
½ cup chopped walnuts
1 teaspoon milk
    Whipped cream, sour cream, or ice cream

Prepare Cinnamon Tart Shell dough. Roll out two-thirds of the dough on a lightly floured surface to a 12-inch circle. Fit into bottom and up side of an 8-inch springform pan. Combine ½ teaspoon cinnamon and 2 teaspoons sugar; sprinkle over crust. Preheat oven to 350° F. Peel, halve, and core pears. Arrange pear halves in crust, hollow-side down and stem ends pointing toward the center. Sprinkle with walnuts. Roll out remaining dough to an 8-inch circle. Cut out a 2½-inch circle in the center of the dough. Cover pears with top crust. Press edges together to seal. Trim and flute edge. Brush with milk. Sprinkle with remaining 1 teaspoon sugar. Bake 45 to 50 minutes or until golden. Serve warm or cold. Before serving, fill center of tart with whipped cream, sour cream, or ice cream.

Cinnamon Tart Shell

    2 cups flour
½ teaspoon salt
2 teaspoons ground cinnamon
⅔ cup vegetable shortening
5 to 6 tablespoons ice water

Combine flour, salt, and cinnamon. Cut in shortening with a pastry blender or two knives until particles are the size of small peas. Sprinkle water, one tablespoon at a time, over flour mixture, tossing lightly with a fork. Gather dough into a ball. Wrap in waxed paper or plastic wrap. Chill 30 minutes or until firm.

Matrimony Pie

Makes 4 to 6 servings

1½ cups peeled, cored, and sliced tart cooking apples
1½ cups peeled, cored, and sliced firm pears
1½ cups seedless green grapes
1 teaspoon lemon juice
¼ cup packed brown sugar
3 tablespoons granulated sugar
3 tablespoons flour
¼ teaspoon grated lemon peel
¼ teaspoon ground cinnamon
⅛ teaspoon ground nutmeg
⅛ teaspoon salt
1 recipe Single Piecrust (page 15)
1 egg white, lightly beaten
Sugar

In a large bowl, combine apples, pears, grapes, and lemon juice; toss lightly to mix. In a small bowl, mix sugars, flour, lemon peel, cinnamon, nutmeg, and salt. Add to fruit; toss lightly. Turn into a 1-quart baking dish. Preheat oven to 425° F. Prepare piecrust dough. Roll out on a floured surface to ¼-inch thickness. Cover fruit with crust. Trim and flute edge. Brush with egg white. Sprinkle lightly with sugar. Bake for 30 minutes or until crust is well browned. Serve warm.

Old-Fashioned Pear Pie

Makes 6 to 8 servings

½ cup sugar
½ cup flour
¼ teaspoon ground mace
½ teaspoon ground cinnamon
11 medium Bartlett pears, peeled and sliced
1 recipe Double Piecrust (page 15)
1 tablespoon butter *or* margarine
1 egg white, lightly beaten
1 tablespoon sugar

In a medium bowl, combine sugar, flour, mace, and cinnamon. Add pears; toss lightly. Preheat oven to 450° F. Prepare piecrust dough. On a lightly floured surface, roll out ½ of the dough to a circle 1 inch larger than an inverted 9-inch pie plate. Fit crust into pie plate. Moisten edge with a little water. Turn pears into crust. Dot with butter. Roll out remaining dough. Cover pears with top crust; seal edges. Trim and flute edge. Brush crust with egg white. Sprinkle with 1 tablespoon sugar. Cut slits in top to vent steam. Bake on lowest shelf of oven for 25 minutes. If edge is browning too rapidly, cover with a strip of aluminum foil. Reduce oven temperature to 375° F.; bake 20 minutes. Cool on a wire rack before cutting.

Cherry Dessert Wontons

Makes 4 dozen

48 wonton wrappers
1 can (29 ounces) cherry pie filling
3 cups vegetable oil
Powdered sugar *or* cinnamon sugar

Fill each wonton wrapper with about 1½ teaspoons cherry pie filling placed in the center of the wrapper. Moisten edges of wrappers; fold diagonally to form triangles. Press together to seal. Pull points at opposite sides together to overlap slightly; moisten with water and press to seal. Heat oil in a deep-fat fryer to 375° F. Deep-fry wontons, 8 to 10 at a time, for about 2 minutes or until crisp and golden. Drain on paper towels. Keep warm in a 250° F. oven or reheat for about 5 minutes in a 450° F. oven. Sprinkle with powdered sugar or cinnamon sugar, if desired.

Cream Puff Heart

Makes 10 to 12 servings

1 recipe Cream Puffs (page 20)
1 package (10 ounces) frozen sliced strawberries, drained
Sifted powdered sugar
Cream Filling (recipe follows)

Cut a 9 x 8-inch heart from a piece of paper. Trace the heart with a pencil onto a large baking sheet. Lightly grease baking sheet. Preheat oven to 400° F. Prepare Cream Puff dough. Drop mixture by tablespoonfuls, with sides touching, to cover the heart outlined on the baking sheet. Bake for 45 minutes or until puffy and golden. Cool on a wire rack in a draft-free place. Carefully cut off the top in one piece. Remove any uncooked dough. Spoon Cream Filling into shell. Cover with sliced strawberries. Replace top. Sprinkle with powdered sugar. Serve immediately.

Cream Filling

1 package (3 ounces) vanilla pudding and pie filling mix
1½ cups milk
1 cup whipping cream, whipped
1 teaspoon vanilla

In a medium saucepan, combine pudding mix and milk. Cook over medium heat, stirring constantly, until mixture comes to a full rolling boil. Remove from heat. Press a piece of plastic wrap directly onto surface of pudding. Refrigerate until cool. Fold in whipped cream and vanilla; blend well.

Cream Puff Heart, this page

Fried Pastries

Makes 16 servings

- ¾ cup chopped dates
- ¼ cup water
- ¼ cup sugar
  - Dash salt
- ¾ cup chopped almonds
- 1 package (8 ounces) refrigerated crescent dinner rolls
- 1 egg yolk
- 1 teaspoon water
- 2 teaspoons sesame seed
  - Vegetable oil

In a medium saucepan, combine dates, water, sugar, and salt. Cook over low heat, stirring frequently until thickened. Let stand until cool. Stir in almonds. Unroll crescent rolls without separating at perforations. Place dough on a lightly floured surface. Fold one rectangle of dough over so that perforations are in opposite directions. Roll out dough to a very thin 14 x 7-inch rectangle. Cut lengthwise in half. Cut each half into four 3½-inch squares. Place a rounded teaspoonful of filling on each square. Moisten edges of dough with a little water. Fold dough over filling to form a triangle; pull down corners to form a crescent. Repeat with remaining dough. Lightly beat egg yolk and water. Brush over pastries. Sprinkle with sesame seed. Heat oil for deep-fat frying to 360° F. Deep-fry pastries, 3 or 4 at a time, about 4 minutes or until golden, turning frequently. Drain on paper towels.

Easy Napoleons

Makes about 12 servings

- ½ package (17¼ ounces) frozen puff pastry
- 1 package (4 ounces) instant chocolate pudding mix
- 1 cup dairy sour cream
- ½ cup milk
- 1 cup powdered sugar
- 1 tablespoon milk
- 1 square (1 ounce) semisweet chocolate, melted with
  - 1 teaspoon vegetable shortening

Remove 1 sheet of frozen puff pastry from package; thaw, folded, 20 minutes. Preheat oven to 350° F. Gently unfold and roll out on a lightly floured surface to an 18 x 11-inch rectangle. Cut crosswise to make six 3 x 11-inch strips. Prick pastry well with a fork. Place pastry on an ungreased baking sheet. Bake 18 to 22 minutes. Let stand until cool. Prepare pudding mix according to package directions, substituting 1 cup sour cream and ½ cup milk. In a small bowl, combine powdered sugar and milk; blend until smooth. Spread icing on top of 2 pastry sheets. Drizzle melted chocolate over frosting in thin lines about 1 inch apart. Gently swirl chocolate with a knife. Spread half of the pudding on 2 of the remaining pastry sheets. Cover each with a second pastry sheet. Spread with remaining pudding. Top with frosted sheets. Chill at least 30 minutes before serving. Cut pastry into serving portions.

Cream Puffs with Cherry Filling

Makes 12 servings

- 1 cup water
- ½ cup butter *or* margarine
- 1 cup flour
- ¼ teaspoon salt
- 4 eggs
  - Custard Filling (recipe follows)
- 1½ cups cherry pie filling
  - Sifted powdered sugar

Preheat oven to 400° F. In a medium saucepan, bring water and butter to boiling. Add flour and salt all at once; beat with a wooden spoon until mixture leaves the side of the pan and forms a ball, about 1 to 2 minutes. Remove from heat. Add eggs, one at a time, beating well after each addition. Beat until shiny and smooth. Drop dough by scant ¼-cupfuls about 3 inches apart onto an ungreased baking sheet. Bake for 35 to 40 minutes or until puffy and golden. Cool on a wire rack in a draft-free place. Cut off tops. Remove any uncooked dough. Spoon Custard Filling into cream puffs. Spoon a heaping tablespoonful of cherry pie filling over custard. Replace tops. Sprinkle with powdered sugar.

Custard Filling

- ⅔ cup sugar
- ¼ cup cornstarch
- ¼ teaspoon salt
- 4 cups milk
- 2 egg yolks, lightly beaten
- ¼ cup butter *or* margarine
- 1 tablespoon vanilla

In a medium saucepan, combine sugar, cornstarch, and salt. Gradually add milk, stirring to dissolve cornstarch. Cook over medium heat, stirring constantly until mixture thickens and boils. Boil and stir 1 minute. Stir about half of the hot milk mixture into egg yolks. Return all to milk mixture. Boil and stir 1 minute. Remove from heat. Stir in butter and vanilla. Cool before filling cream puffs.

Cheesecakes and Tortes

Strawberry Topped Cheesecake

Makes 12 servings

    2 cups graham cracker crumbs
1¾ cups sugar, divided
½ cup butter or margarine, melted
    2 packages (8 ounces each) cream cheese, softened
    1 carton (16 ounces) cream-style cottage cheese, sieved
    2 teaspoons vanilla
½ teaspoon salt
    6 eggs, separated
⅓ cup flour
    1 pint strawberries, hulled; reserve ½ cup
    Strawberry Glaze (recipe follows)

In a bowl, combine graham cracker crumbs, ¼ cup sugar, and butter; blend well. Press crumb mixture firmly onto bottom and up side of a 9-inch springform pan. Refrigerate until needed. Preheat oven to 350° F. In a large mixing bowl, combine cheeses; beat until smooth. Blend in remaining 1½ cups sugar, vanilla, and salt. Add egg yolks, one at a time, beating well after each addition. Blend in flour. In a separate large mixing bowl, beat egg whites until stiff but not dry. Pour into prepared pan. Bake 1½ hours. Turn off heat, open oven door, and let cheesecake stand in oven at least 1 hour. Chill 3 to 4 hours before serving. Prepare Strawberry Glaze. Slice strawberries; arrange on top of cheesecake. Brush glaze over berries. Chill until glaze sets.

Strawberry Glaze

½ cup reserved strawberries
    1 cup sugar
¾ cup water, divided
    2 tablespoons lemon juice
    2 tablespoons cornstarch

In a small saucepan, combine berries and sugar; mash berries with a fork. Add ½ cup water and lemon juice. Bring to boiling; reduce heat. Dissolve cornstarch in remaining ¼ cup water. Add to strawberry mixture, stirring constantly until thickened. Remove from heat, strain, and cool.

Red Pie Cherry Cheesecake Tarts

Makes about 30 servings

    Tart Shells (recipe follows)
    2 packages (3 ounces each) cream cheese, softened
¼ cup powdered sugar
    1 tablespoon orange-flavored liqueur
    1 can (16 ounces) red cherries, drained; reserve liquid
    2 or 3 tablespoons granulated sugar
    4 teaspoons cornstarch
    Dash salt
    1 drop red food coloring, optional

Prepare Tart Shells; set aside. In a large mixing bowl, combine cream cheese, powdered sugar, and liqueur; beat until light and fluffy. Spoon or pipe with a pastry bag about 1 teaspoon cheese mixture into each tart shell. Measure reserved cherry liquid. Add water, if necessary, to equal ¾ cup. In a small saucepan, combine cherry liquid, granulated sugar, cornstarch, and salt; add red food coloring, if desired. Stir to dissolve cornstarch. Cook over medium heat, stirring constantly until thickened and clear; cool slightly. Place 2 cherries on top of filling in each tart shell. Spoon glaze over tops.

Tart Shells

Makes about 39 shells

    2 cups flour
¼ cup sugar
½ teaspoon finely grated orange peel
¾ cup butter or margarine
    1 egg, lightly beaten

Preheat oven to 400° F. Stir together flour, sugar, and orange peel. Cut in butter with a pastry blender or two knives until particles are the size of small peas. Blend in egg with fingers until mixture forms a ball. Press a scant tablespoon of dough into 2-inch round tart pans. Place pans on a baking sheet. Bake 12 to 14 minutes or until golden. Cool in pans.

Pumpkin Cheesecake with Cherry Topping

Makes 15 servings

　　2 tablespoons butter *or* margarine
　¼ cup graham cracker crumbs
　¼ cup finely chopped pecans
　　4 packages (8 ounces each) cream cheese, softened
　⅓ cup flour
1½ cups sugar
1½ tablespoons pumpkin pie spice
　⅛ teaspoon salt
　　6 eggs
　　2 cups canned pumpkin
　　1 can (29 ounces) cherry pie filling

Preheat oven to 325° F. Butter bottom and side of a 12-inch springform pan. Sprinkle with graham cracker crumbs and nuts; tilt pan to coat all sides. Tap out excess. In a large mixing bowl, beat cream cheese until fluffy. Add flour, sugar, spice, and salt; blend well. Add eggs, one at a time, beating well after each addition. Add pumpkin; blend well. Pour batter into prepared pan. Bake for 1½ hours. Cool to room temperature. Chill for at least 2 hours. Spread cherry pie filling over top.

Cherry Chocolate Cheesecake Squares

Makes 20 servings

　　1 recipe Double Piecrust (page 15)
　　2 eggs
　　4 packages (3 ounces each) cream cheese, softened
　¾ cup sugar
　¼ cup unsweetened cocoa
　¼ teaspoon almond extract
　　1 cup dairy sour cream
　　1 can (17 ounces) dark sweet cherries, drained and chopped
　½ cup blanched sliced almonds
　　　Whipped cream

Prepare piecrust dough. Crumble dough into the bottom of a 15 x 11-inch baking pan. Press evenly over bottom and up sides of pan. Prick well with a fork. Bake at 400° F. for 10 minutes. Remove from oven; set aside. Reduce heat to 350° F. In a blender or food processor, blend eggs, cream cheese, sugar, cocoa, and almond extract until very smooth. Pour into a bowl. Stir in sour cream and chopped cherries. Pour cheese mixture into prepared crust. Sprinkle with almonds. Bake for 30 to 35 minutes or until edge is set. Cool to room temperature. Chill 3 to 4 hours. Cut into 3-inch squares. Top with whipped cream.

Perfect Cheesecake with Blueberry Topping

Makes 12 servings

　　2 packages (8 ounces each) cream cheese, softened
　　1 carton (16 ounces) cream-style cottage cheese
1½ cups sugar
　　4 eggs
　　3 tablespoons cornstarch
1½ tablespoons lemon juice
　　1 tablespoon vanilla
　¼ pound butter, melted and cooled
　　2 cups dairy sour cream
　　1 can (21 ounces) blueberry pie filling

Preheat oven to 325° F. Lightly butter a 9-inch springform pan. In a large mixing bowl, combine cheeses; beat until light and fluffy. Add sugar; blend well. Add eggs, one at a time, beating well after each addition. Add cornstarch, lemon juice, vanilla, and butter; blend until smooth. Blend in sour cream. Pour batter into prepared pan. Bake for 1 hour 10 minutes or until center is set. Turn oven off. Let cheesecake stand in oven, with the door closed, for 2 hours. Cool completely. Chill 6 hours. Spoon blueberry pie filling on top.

Pineapple Cheesecake

Makes 12 servings

1¾ cups graham cracker crumbs
　¾ cup sugar, divided
　½ cup butter *or* margarine, melted
　　4 packages (3 ounces each) cream cheese, softened
1½ teaspoons vanilla, divided
　½ cup sugar
　⅛ teaspoon ground cinnamon
　　2 eggs, lightly beaten
　　1 can (20 ounces) crushed pineapple, drained
　　1 cup dairy sour cream
　　3 tablespoons sugar

Preheat oven to 325° F. In a small bowl, combine crumbs, ¼ cup sugar, and butter; blend well. Press firmly onto bottom and side of a 9-inch springform pan or a quiche or tart pan with a removable bottom. In a large mixing bowl, combine cream cheese, ½ teaspoon vanilla, remaining ½ cup sugar, and cinnamon; beat until light and fluffy. Add eggs; blend well. Stir in pineapple. Pour into prepared pan. Bake for 35 minutes or until center is set. While cheesecake is baking, mix sour cream, 3 tablespoons sugar, and remaining 1 teaspoon vanilla. Remove cheesecake from oven. Spread sour cream mixture on top. Cool to room temperature. Chill well before serving.

Perfect Cheesecake with Blueberry Topping, this page

Rum Fruit Torte

Makes 10 servings

        4 eggs, separated
    ⅔ cup sugar
    ¼ cup water
        1 teaspoon vanilla
    ¼ teaspoon almond extract
    ⅔ cup sifted cake flour
    ¾ teaspoon baking powder
    ¼ teaspoon salt
        Rum Filling (recipe follows)
        Sliced peaches
        Sliced strawberries
    1½ cups whipping cream, whipped

Preheat oven to 325° F. In a mixing bowl, beat egg yolks until light-colored. Gradually blend in sugar. Add water, vanilla, and almond extract. In a separate bowl, sift together flour, baking powder, and salt. Blend into egg mixture with a wire whisk. In a small mixing bowl, beat egg whites until stiff but not dry. Fold egg whites into egg mixture. Turn into an ungreased 9-inch springform or tube pan. Bake for 50 to 55 minutes or until a wooden pick inserted near the center comes out clean. Invert pan onto a wire rack. Cool completely in pan. Loosen edge of cake with a spatula or knife. Cut into 3 layers. Place one layer on a cake plate. Spread with half of the Rum Filling. Top with sliced peaches. Place second layer on top of peaches. Spread with remaining Rum Filling. Top with sliced strawberries. Spread sides and top with whipped cream. Garnish with sliced peaches and strawberries. Serve immediately or chill until serving time.

Rum Filling

        2 teaspoons unflavored gelatin
        2 tablespoons cold water
    ½ cup milk
        2 egg yolks
    ⅓ cup sugar
        3 tablespoons rum
    ¼ teaspoon vanilla
        Dash salt
    ½ cup whipping cream, whipped

Sprinkle gelatin over water; let stand 5 minutes to soften gelatin. In a saucepan, scald milk. Add gelatin; stir until gelatin dissolves. In a mixing bowl, lightly beat egg yolks. Add sugar; blend well. Stir in hot milk mixture. Stir in rum, vanilla, and salt. Chill until slightly thickened. Fold in whipped cream. Fold in egg whites. Chill until almost set.

Schaum Torte

Makes 12 servings

    1⅓ cups egg whites (about 9)
        3 cups sugar
    1½ teaspoons cider vinegar
        2 teaspoons vanilla
    ⅜ teaspoon salt
        2 cups crushed strawberries
        Sugar
        1 cup whipping cream

Grease bottom and side of a 10-inch springform pan; set aside. In a large mixing bowl, combine egg whites, sugar, vinegar, vanilla, and salt; beat on low speed until foamy. Beat on high speed 10 to 15 minutes or until stiff peaks form a meringue. Preheat oven to 500° F. Pour meringue into prepared pan. Place in oven. Turn off heat. Leave pan in oven, with door closed, for 5 hours. Sweeten strawberries with sugar to taste. In a small mixing bowl, beat whipping cream with sugar to taste until stiff. Serve torte topped with strawberries and whipped cream.

Banana Split Torte

Makes 12 servings

    1½ cups butter *or* margarine, divided
        1 cup flour
    ½ cup finely ground nuts
        2 eggs
        2 cups powdered sugar
        3 or 4 bananas
        1 can (20 ounces) crushed pineapple, drained; reserve juice
        2 packages (10 ounces each) frozen strawberries, thawed and drained *or* 2 cups sliced fresh strawberries
        2 cups whipping cream, whipped
        Chopped nuts
        Maraschino cherry halves

Preheat oven to 375° F. In a small bowl, combine ½ cup butter, flour, and ground nuts; blend well. Press firmly onto bottom of a 13 x 9-inch baking pan. Bake for 10 minutes. Remove from oven; set aside to cool. In a large mixing bowl, combine eggs, remaining 1 cup butter, and powdered sugar; beat 15 minutes on medium speed. Spread over cooled crust. Peel and slice bananas; dip in reserved pineapple juice. Arrange bananas on top of filling. Cover with pineapple. Arrange strawberries on top of pineapple; top with whipped cream. Sprinkle with chopped nuts and cherry halves. Chill at least 4 hours.

Walnut Rum Torte

Makes 10 servings

       6 eggs, separated
   ½ teaspoon salt
   3 tablespoons powdered sugar
   1 cup granulated sugar
   1 tablespoon vanilla
   1⅔ cups sifted flour
   ⅓ cup butter *or* margarine, melted and cooled
   1 cup chopped walnuts, divided
       Rum Sauce (recipe follows)

Grease and flour a 9-inch ring mold or tube pan; set aside. Preheat oven to 350° F. In a small mixing bowl, beat egg whites and salt until soft peaks form. Gradually add powdered sugar; beat until stiff but not dry. In a separate bowl, beat egg yolks until light-colored. Add sugar and vanilla; beat until thick and creamy. Sift flour over egg whites. Add yolks; gently fold ingredients until partially blended. Add butter and ¾ cup walnuts; fold until just mixed. Pour into prepared pan. Sprinkle with remaining ¼ cup nuts. Bake for 40 minutes or until a wooden pick inserted near the center comes out clean. Cool in pan while preparing Rum Sauce. Poke holes in top of cake with a long skewer. Spoon sauce over cake. Let stand about 10 minutes to absorb sauce. Turn cake out onto a serving plate.

Rum Sauce

   1½ cups sugar
   1¼ cups water
       Dash salt
       Grated peel of ½ orange
       Grated peel of ½ lemon
   ¼ to ½ cup dark rum

In a medium saucepan, combine all ingredients; bring to boiling. Boil 10 minutes. Cool.

Purple Plum Torte

Makes 12 servings

   1 package (18½ ounces) lemon cake mix
   4 eggs
   1 cup dairy sour cream
   1½ cups coarsely diced purple prune plums
   7 whole purple prune plums
       Powdered sugar
       Cream Cheese Topping (recipe follows)

Grease and flour a 10-inch tube or Bundt pan; set aside. Preheat oven to 350° F. Prepare cake mix with eggs and sour cream, following package directions; beat 3 minutes on medium speed.

Stir in diced plums. Cut 7 plums in halves. Arrange halves, skin-sides down, in prepared pan. Pour cake batter over plums. Bake for 40 to 45 minutes or until cake springs back when pressed lightly near center. Cool in pan 5 minutes before turning out onto a wire rack to cool completely. Sprinkle with powdered sugar. Serve with Cream Cheese Topping.

Cream Cheese Topping

   1 package (3 ounces) cream cheese, softened
   ½ cup dairy sour cream
   2 tablespoons powdered sugar
   2 teaspoons grated orange peel

In a small bowl, combine all ingredients; blend well. Chill before serving.

Raspberry Sour Cream Torte

Makes 8 to 10 servings

       Torte Crust (recipe follows)
   1 can (16 ounces) raspberries, drained; reserve syrup
   1½ tablespoons cornstarch
   ¼ teaspoon ground cinnamon
   1 egg, lightly beaten
   1½ cups dairy sour cream
   ⅓ cup sugar
   1 teaspoon vanilla

Prepare Torte Crust; set aside. Preheat oven to 350° F. Combine reserved raspberry syrup with cornstarch and cinnamon; stir to dissolve cornstarch. Cook over medium heat, stirring constantly until thickened. Stir in berries. Pour berry mixture into crust. In a small bowl, combine egg, sour cream, sugar, and vanilla; blend well. Spoon over fruit filling. Bake for 65 minutes or until edge is lightly browned and topping along edge is dull. Cool to room temperature. Chill well.

Torte Crust

   ½ cup butter *or* margarine
   3 tablespoons sugar
   1 egg
   1½ cups flour
   ¾ teaspoon baking powder
   ¼ teaspoon salt

Preheat oven to 400° F. In a mixing bowl, cream butter and sugar until smooth. Add egg; beat until fluffy. In a separate bowl, mix flour, baking powder, and salt. Gradually add to butter mixture, beating well. Press two-thirds of the flour mixture onto bottom of a 9-inch springform pan. Bake 10 minutes or until golden. Cool. Press remaining flour mixture onto side of pan.

Cookies, Bars, and Brownies

Chocolate Peanut Butter Layered Cookies

Makes about 3 dozen

- ½ cup butter *or* margarine
- ⅓ cup creamy peanut butter
- ½ cup sugar
- ¼ cup packed brown sugar
- 1 egg
- 2 tablespoons milk
- 1 teaspoon vanilla
- 2¼ cups flour
- ¼ teaspoon baking powder
- ¼ teaspoon salt
- 2 squares (1 ounce each) unsweetened baking chocolate, melted and cooled
- Dark Chocolate Glaze (recipe follows)

In a large mixing bowl, cream butter and peanut butter until smooth. Gradually add sugars, beating until light and fluffy. Blend in egg, milk, and vanilla. In a separate bowl, stir together flour, baking powder, and salt. Gradually add flour mixture to creamed mixture; blend well. Divide dough into two equal parts. Thoroughly blend cooled chocolate into one part. Divide each dough in half. Roll out each of the 4 parts between sheets of waxed paper to make four 8-inch squares. Removing the waxed paper, layer light and dark doughs. Cover and chill 4 hours or until firm. Preheat oven to 350° F. Cut dough into 2-inch bars. Place bars on ungreased baking sheets. Bake for 12 to 14 minutes or until lightly browned. Remove from baking sheets to a wire rack to cool. Drizzle with Dark Chocolate Glaze.

Dark Chocolate Glaze

- 5 ounces semisweet chocolate, coarsely chopped
- 1 ounce unsweetened baking chocolate, coarsely chopped
- ¼ cup sugar
- ¼ cup hot coffee
- 2 tablespoons butter

In the top of a double boiler, melt chocolate over hot but not boiling water. Dissolve sugar in hot coffee. Stir into chocolate. Stir in butter until smooth.

Date Nut Pinwheels

Makes about 5 dozen

- 2¼ cups pitted dates, cut up
- 1 cup granulated sugar
- 1 cup water
- 1 cup chopped nuts
- 1 cup vegetable shortening
- 2 cups packed brown sugar
- 3 eggs, well beaten
- 4 cups sifted flour
- ½ teaspoon salt
- ½ teaspoon baking soda

In a small saucepan, combine dates, granulated sugar, and water. Cook over low heat, stirring constantly until thickened. Stir in nuts. Let stand until cool. In a large mixing bowl, cream shortening and brown sugar until light and fluffy. Add eggs; blend well. Gradually add flour, salt, and baking soda; blend well. Cover and chill until dough is stiff. Divide dough in half. Roll out each half into a rectangle slightly less than ¼ inch thick. Spread each half with date filling. Roll up from long side, jelly-roll fashion. Wrap in waxed paper or plastic wrap. Chill 8 hours or overnight. Grease a large baking sheet. Preheat oven to 400° F. Cut roll into slices ¼ inch thick; place about 2 inches apart on ungreased baking sheets. Bake for 10 to 12 minutes or until golden. Remove from baking sheets to a wire rack to cool.

Coconut Kisses

Makes 2 dozen

- 2 egg whites
- 1 cup sugar
- 1 can (3½ ounces) flaked coconut

Preheat oven to 250° F. In a small mixing bowl, beat egg whites until stiff but not dry. Gradually add sugar, beating until stiff peaks form. Fold in coconut. Drop batter by teaspoonfuls onto an ungreased baking sheet. Bake for 25 minutes or until lightly golden.

Candy Cane Cookies

Makes about 3 dozen

½ **cup vegetable shortening**
½ **cup butter** *or* **margarine**
2 **cups sifted powdered sugar**
1 **egg**
1½ **teaspoons vanilla**
1½ **teaspoons almond extract**
2½ **cups flour**
½ **teaspoon salt**
1 **teaspoon red food coloring**
½ **cup crushed peppermint candies**
½ **cup sugar**

Preheat oven to 375° F. In a large mixing bowl, cream shortening, butter, powdered sugar, egg, vanilla, and almond extract until light and fluffy. In a separate bowl, stir together flour and salt. Gradually add flour to creamed mixture. Divide dough into two equal parts. Blend one part with red food coloring. Blend the remaining part with peppermint candies. For each cookie, roll two 5-inch strips. Use 1 teaspoon of tinted dough for one strip, and 1 teaspoon of dough with candies for the other. Press the two strips together lightly and twist to make a rope. Repeat for remaining dough. Place candy canes on a large baking sheet. Sprinkle with ½ cup sugar. Bake for 8 to 10 minutes or until firm. Remove from baking sheet to wire racks to cool.

Cherry Topped Christmas Cookies

Makes about 3 dozen

½ **cup vegetable shortening**
¼ **cup sugar**
1 **egg, separated**
1 **tablespoon grated orange peel**
1½ **teaspoons grated lemon peel**
½ **teaspoon vanilla**
1 **tablespoon lemon juice**
1 **cup sifted cake flour**
¾ **cup chopped nuts**
6 **candied cherries, cut in small pieces**

In a large mixing bowl, cream shortening and sugar until light and fluffy. Add egg yolk, orange and lemon peel, vanilla, and lemon juice; blend well. Gradually blend in flour. Cover and chill at least 4 hours. Preheat oven to 350° F. Shape dough into ½-inch balls; roll in lightly beaten egg white, then in chopped nuts. Place balls on greased baking sheets. Press a cherry piece on top of each ball. Bake for 20 minutes or until lightly browned. Remove from baking sheets to wire racks to cool.

Applesauce Spice Cookies

Makes about 3 dozen

½ **cup vegetable shortening**
½ **cup sugar**
1 **egg**
1 **cup applesauce**
1¾ **cups flour**
1 **teaspoon baking soda**
½ **teaspoon baking powder**
½ **teaspoon salt**
1 **teaspoon ground cinnamon**
½ **teaspoon ground cloves**
½ **teaspoon ground nutmeg**
1 **cup quick-cooking oats**
½ **cup raisins**
½ **cup chopped nuts**

Preheat oven to 350° F. In a large mixing bowl, cream shortening and sugar until light and fluffy. Blend in egg, then applesauce. In a separate bowl, stir together flour, baking soda, baking powder, salt, cinnamon, cloves, and nutmeg. Gradually add dry ingredients to applesauce mixture; blend well. Stir in oats, raisins, and nuts. Drop by tablespoonfuls onto greased baking sheets. Bake for 15 minutes or until lightly browned. Remove from baking sheets to a wire rack to cool.

Chocolate Coffee Drops

Makes about 4 dozen

2¼ **cups flour**
1 **tablespoon baking powder**
1 **teaspoon salt**
2 **teaspoons ground nutmeg**
2 **teaspoons ground cinnamon**
2 **tablespoons boiling water**
2 **tablespoons instant coffee powder**
⅔ **cup vegetable shortening**
1 **cup packed dark brown sugar**
1 **egg**
1 **teaspoon vanilla**
1 **package (12 ounces) semisweet chocolate chips**
½ **cup chopped nuts**

Preheat oven to 350° F. Stir together flour, baking powder, salt, nutmeg, and cinnamon. Combine boiling water and coffee; set aside to cool. In a large mixing bowl, cream shortening and sugar until light and fluffy. Add egg and vanilla; blend well. Alternately add dry ingredients and cooled coffee to creamed mixture, blending well after each addition. Stir in chocolate chips and nuts. Drop by level tablespoonfuls onto greased baking sheets. Bake for 6 to 8 minutes or until lightly browned. Remove from baking sheets to a wire rack to cool.

Jamwiches

Makes about 2 dozen

⅔ cup vegetable shortening
¾ cup sugar
1 egg
1 teaspoon vanilla
2 cups flour
1½ teaspoons baking powder
¼ teaspoon salt
4 teaspoons milk
Tart red jelly
Pink Icing (recipe follows)

In a large mixing bowl, cream shortening and sugar until light and fluffy. Add egg and vanilla; blend well. In a separate bowl, stir together flour, baking powder, and salt. Blend flour, then milk, into creamed mixture. Divide dough in half. Cover and chill 1 hour. Preheat oven to 375° F. Roll out each half on a lightly floured surface to ⅛-inch thickness. Cut out one half with a 3-inch cookie cutter; cut out the other half with a 3-inch dough-nut cutter. Place on greased baking sheets. Bake for 7 to 10 minutes or until lightly browned. Remove from baking sheets to a wire rack to cool. Spread whole cookies with jelly. Top with remaining cookies. Frost tops with Pink Icing.

Pink Icing

1 cup sifted powdered sugar
1½ tablespoons milk
1½ teaspoons butter *or* margarine, softened
¼ teaspoon vanilla
Red food coloring

In a small mixing bowl, combine powdered sugar, milk, butter, and vanilla; beat until smooth. Tint with red food coloring; blend well.

Peanut Crunchies

Makes about 5 dozen

1 cup butter *or* margarine
½ cup packed brown sugar
2 eggs, separated
1 teaspoon vanilla
2 cups flour
1 teaspoon salt
2 cups chopped salted peanuts
½ cup peanut butter
½ cup apple jelly

Preheat oven to 375° F. In a large mixing bowl, cream butter and sugar until light and fluffy. Add egg yolks and vanilla; blend well. In a separate bowl, stir together flour and salt; gradually blend into creamed mixture. Shape dough into 1-inch balls. In a small bowl, lightly beat egg whites. Dip balls in egg whites, then roll in peanuts. Place on ungreased baking sheets. Bake for 5 minutes. Remove baking sheet from oven. Press thumb gently into tops of cookies. Return to oven for 8 minutes. Remove from baking sheets to a wire rack to cool. Blend peanut butter and jelly. Fill centers of cookies with peanut butter and jelly mixture.

Pistachio Cookies

Makes about 4 dozen

1 cup vegetable shortening
½ cup powdered sugar
1 teaspoon vanilla
½ teaspoon grated lime peel
2¼ cups flour
½ teaspoon salt
½ cup finely chopped pistachio nuts
Powdered sugar

Preheat oven to 400° F. In a large mixing bowl, cream shortening, ½ cup powdered sugar, vanilla, and lime peel until light and fluffy. Gradually add flour, salt, and pistachios; blend well. Shape dough into 1-inch balls. Place balls about 2 inches apart on ungreased baking sheets. Bake for 8 to 10 minutes or until firm but not browned. Remove from baking sheets to a wire rack to cool. When cool enough to handle, dip tops in powdered sugar.

Tea Cookies

Makes about 5 dozen

1 cup butter
⅔ cup sugar
3 egg yolks
3 cups cake flour
1 teaspoon almond extract
Yellow, red, or green food coloring

In a large mixing bowl, cream butter and sugar until light and fluffy. Add egg yolks, one at a time, beating well after each addition. Gradually add flour and almond extract; blend well. Divide dough into thirds. Tint each portion with food coloring, blending well. Shape into 2-inch rolls. Wrap in waxed paper or plastic wrap. Chill 3 to 4 hours or until firm. Preheat oven to 400° F. Cut rolls into slices ¼ inch thick; place about 2 inches apart on ungreased baking sheets. Bake 8 to 10 minutes or until lightly browned. Remove from baking sheets to a wire rack to cool.

Pineapple Squares

Makes 16 squares

¼ cup butter *or* margarine, melted
1¾ cups sugar
4 eggs
1½ cups flour
½ teaspoon salt
½ teaspoon baking soda
1 can (16 ounces) crushed pineapple, drained
1 cup chopped nuts

Grease a 13 x 9-inch baking pan. Preheat oven to 350° F. In a large mixing bowl, cream butter and sugar until smooth. Add eggs, one at a time, beating well after each addition. In a separate bowl, sift together flour, salt, and baking soda. Gradually add dry ingredients to creamed mixture; blend well. Stir in pineapple and nuts. Press into prepared pan. Bake for 40 minutes or until golden. Cool slightly in pan.

Chocolate Chip Butterscotch Squares

Makes about 36 squares

⅔ cup vegetable shortening, melted
2¼ cups packed brown sugar
3 eggs
1 teaspoon vanilla
2¾ cups sifted flour
2½ teaspoons baking powder
½ teaspoon salt
1 package (6 ounces) semisweet chocolate chips

Grease a 15 x 10-inch baking pan. Preheat oven to 350° F. Cream shortening and brown sugar until smooth. Add eggs, one at a time, beating well after each addition. Add vanilla; blend well. In a separate bowl, stir together flour, baking powder, and salt. Gradually blend dry ingredients into creamed mixture. Stir in chocolate chips. Spread batter in prepared pan. Bake for 20 minutes or until lightly browned. Cool slightly in pan.

Pecan Pie Bars

Makes 16 bars

2 cups flour
1 cup packed brown sugar
½ cup butter
½ cup margarine
5 eggs
1 cup dark corn syrup
¾ cup granulated sugar
Dash salt
1 teaspoon vanilla
1 cup broken pecans

Preheat oven to 350° F. In a large mixing bowl, combine flour and brown sugar. Cut in butter and margarine with a pastry blender or two knives until mixture resembles coarse crumbs. Press crumb mixture into a 13 x 9-inch baking pan. Bake for 10 minutes or until golden. While crust is baking, combine eggs, corn syrup, granulated sugar, salt, and vanilla; blend well. Stir in pecans. Pour filling over hot crust. Reduce oven temperature to 275° F. Bake about 50 minutes or until center is set. Cool in pan on a wire rack before cutting into bars.

Chocolate Mint Bars

Makes 16 bars

⅔ cup vegetable shortening
2 cups packed brown sugar
3 eggs
1 teaspoon vanilla
1½ cups flour
½ cup unsweetened cocoa
1 teaspoon salt
1 teaspoon baking powder
Mint Frosting (recipe follows)
Chocolate Glaze (recipe follows)

Grease a 13 x 9-inch baking pan. Preheat oven to 350° F. In a large mixing bowl, cream shortening and brown sugar until smooth. Add eggs, one at a time, beating well after each addition. Blend in vanilla. In a separate bowl, stir together flour, cocoa, salt, and baking powder. Gradually add to creamed mixture; blend well. Spread in the prepared baking pan. Bake for 25 to 30 minutes or until brownie just begins to pull away from edge of pan. Cool in pan on a wire rack. Frost with Mint Frosting. Chill until firm. Drizzle with Chocolate Glaze. Let stand until set. Cut into bars.

Mint Frosting

2 cups powdered sugar
2 tablespoons milk
½ cup butter *or* margarine, softened
½ teaspoon peppermint flavoring

In a small bowl, combine all ingredients; blend well.

Chocolate Glaze

1 cup semisweet chocolate chips
6 tablespoons butter *or* margarine

In a small saucepan, combine chocolate chips and butter. Melt over low heat, stirring constantly until smooth.

Chocolate Nut Brownies, 48

Butterscotch Brownies

Makes 18 brownies

- ¼ cup butter *or* margarine
- 1 cup packed brown sugar
- 1 egg, lightly beaten
- ½ cup flour
- 1 teaspoon baking powder
- ½ teaspoon salt
- ½ teaspoon vanilla
- ½ cup chopped nuts

Grease an 8-inch square baking pan. Preheat oven to 350° F. In a medium saucepan, melt butter over low heat. Remove from heat and stir in sugar; let stand until cool. Blend in egg. In a separate bowl, combine flour, baking powder, and salt. Gradually add to butter mixture, blending well. Stir in vanilla and nuts. Spread in prepared pan. Bake 20 minutes. Cool slightly in pan before cutting into bars.

Triple Decker Brownies

Makes 24 brownies

- 1 cup butter *or* margarine, melted
- 1 cup packed brown sugar
- 1 cup flour
- ½ teaspoon baking soda
- 2 cups rolled oats
  - Chocolate Nut Dough (recipe follows)
  - Chocolate Mocha Frosting (recipe follows)

Grease and flour a 15 x 12-inch baking pan; set aside. Preheat oven to 350° F. In a large mixing bowl, cream butter and brown sugar until smooth. Gradually add flour and baking soda; blend well. Stir in oatmeal. Press dough into the prepared baking pan. Bake for 10 minutes or until golden. Remove from oven. Spread with Chocolate Nut Dough. Return to oven. Bake for 18 to 20 minutes or until golden. Remove from oven to a wire rack to cool. Frost with Chocolate Mocha Frosting. Cut into squares.

Chocolate Nut Dough

- ½ cup vegetable shortening
- 1¼ cups sugar
- 4 eggs
- 1 cup flour
- 4 heaping tablespoons unsweetened cocoa
- ½ teaspoon salt
- 1 teaspoon vanilla
- ½ cup chopped nuts

In a large mixing bowl, cream shortening and sugar until smooth. Add eggs, one at a time, beating well after each addition. In a small bowl, stir together flour, cocoa, and salt. Gradually add to creamed mixture; blend well. Blend in vanilla. Stir in nuts.

Chocolate Mocha Frosting

- ¼ cup hot coffee
- ¼ cup butter *or* margarine
- ¼ cup unsweetened cocoa
- 1 teaspoon vanilla
- 2 cups sifted powdered sugar

In a small mixing bowl, pour hot coffee over butter; stir until butter melts. Blend in cocoa and vanilla. Gradually beat in powdered sugar until smooth.

Praline Bars

Makes 36 bars

- ⅓ cup butter *or* margarine, softened
- 1¼ cups packed brown sugar
- 1 egg
- 2 tablespoons milk
- 1 teaspoon vanilla
- 1½ cups flour
- 1 teaspoon baking powder
- ¼ teaspoon salt
- ½ cup broken pecans
  - Praline Frosting (recipe follows)

Grease a 13 x 9-inch baking pan. Preheat oven to 350° F. In a large mixing bowl, cream butter and brown sugar; blend in egg, milk, and vanilla. In a separate bowl, stir together flour, baking powder, and salt. Gradually add to creamed mixture; blend well. Dough will be very stiff. Spread in prepared pan. Sprinkle with pecans. Bake for 25 to 30 minutes or until lightly browned. Cool in pan. Drizzle with Praline Frosting and cut into bars.

Praline Frosting

- ½ cup packed brown sugar
- 2 tablespoons butter *or* margarine
- 1 tablespoon milk
- ½ cup sifted powdered sugar

In a small saucepan, combine brown sugar, butter, and milk. Cook over low heat until butter melts, stirring constantly. Remove from heat. Stir in powdered sugar; beat until smooth. Drizzle warm frosting on bars.

Candies and Confections

Oh-So-Easy Caramels

Makes about 2½ pounds

    1 cup butter *or* margarine
    1 pound brown sugar
      Dash salt
    1 cup light corn syrup
    1 can (14 ounces) sweetened condensed milk
    1 teaspoon vanilla

Butter a 9-inch square baking pan; set aside. In a heavy, 3-quart saucepan, melt butter. Add brown sugar and salt; blend well. Stir in corn syrup, then gradually stir in milk until blended. Cook over medium heat, stirring constantly about 12 to 15 minutes, or until mixture reaches 245° F. on a candy thermometer. Remove from heat. Stir in vanilla. Pour into prepared pan. Cool before cutting into squares. Wrap each caramel in plastic wrap.

Mock Baby Ruth Bars

Makes 16 to 20 servings

    ⅔ cup margarine
    1 cup packed brown sugar
    ¼ cup light *or* dark corn syrup
    ¼ cup crunchy peanut butter
    1 teaspoon vanilla
    4 cups quick-cooking rolled oats
    1 package (12 ounces) milk chocolate chips
    1 package (6 ounces) butterscotch chips
    ⅔ cup smooth *or* crunchy peanut butter
    1 cup salted Spanish peanuts

Grease a 13 x 9-inch baking pan; set aside. Preheat oven to 375° F. In a medium saucepan, combine margarine, brown sugar, and corn syrup. Cook over low heat, stirring constantly until margarine is melted. Stir in ¼ cup peanut butter and vanilla. In a large bowl, combine oatmeal and peanut butter mixture; blend well. Press firmly into prepared pan. Bake for 12 minutes. Remove from oven. In a saucepan, combine chocolate and butterscotch chips; cook over low heat, stirring constantly until chips melt. Stir in remaining ⅔ cup peanut butter and peanuts. Pour over baked crust. Cool before cutting into pieces.

Nearly Nut Goodie Bars

Makes 48 servings

    1 package (12 ounces) semisweet chocolate chips
    1 package (12 ounces) butterscotch chips
    1 jar (18 ounces) peanut butter
    1 jar (16 ounces) dry roasted peanuts
    1 cup butter *or* margarine
    ½ cup milk
    ¼ cup vanilla pudding mix
    1 bag (2 pounds) powdered sugar
    1 tablespoon maple flavoring

Butter a 15 x 12-inch baking pan; set aside. In a large saucepan, melt chocolate and butterscotch chips. Stir in peanut butter until smooth. Spread half of the mixture in prepared pan. Chill about 1 hour or until firm. Stir peanuts into remaining chocolate mixture; set aside. In a large saucepan, combine butter, milk, and pudding mix. Bring to boiling, stirring constantly; boil 1 minute. Remove from heat. Gradually beat in powdered sugar and maple flavoring. Spread over mixture in pan. Spread with chocolate-peanut mixture. Chill before cutting into pieces.

Almond Toffee

Makes about 1 pound

    1 cup sliced blanched almonds, divided
    1 cup butter
    1 cup sugar
    2 tablespoons water
    1 tablespoon white corn syrup
    ¼ teaspoon salt
    ½ teaspoon vanilla
    1 bar (8 ounces) milk chocolate, coarsely chopped

Line a large baking sheet with aluminum foil. Sprinkle ¾ cup nuts over foil; set aside. In a heavy skillet, melt butter. Remove from heat. Add sugar, stirring until sugar dissolves. Stir in water, corn syrup, and salt. Cook mixture over medium heat to 293° F. on a candy thermometer, stirring occasionally. Stir in vanilla. Pour over nuts in pan. Sprinkle chocolate over top. Sprinkle with remaining nuts. Let stand until cool. Break candy into pieces.

Almost O'Henry Bars

Makes 12 to 16 servings

  ½ cup peanut butter
  ½ cup packed brown sugar
  ½ cup light corn syrup
  2 cups cornflake cereal
  1 cup crispy rice cereal
  ½ cup margarine
  2 tablespoons vanilla pudding mix
  2 cups powdered sugar
  4 squares (1 ounce each) semisweet baking chocolate
  2 tablespoons margarine

In a bowl, combine peanut butter, brown sugar, corn syrup, and cereals; blend well. Spread in a 9-inch square baking pan, using a wooden spoon dipped in water. In a small saucepan, melt ½ cup margarine. Stir in pudding mix. Gradually add powdered sugar, stirring until smooth. Spread over the cereal mixture. In a small saucepan, melt chocolate and 2 tablespoons margarine, stirring constantly. Drizzle chocolate mixture over the top. Chill before cutting into pieces.

Rocky Road Fudge

Makes about 40 squares

  1 package (12 ounces) semisweet chocolate chips
  1 can (14 ounces) sweetened condensed milk
  2 tablespoons margarine
  2 cups dry roasted peanuts
  1 package (10½ ounces) miniature marshmallows

Line a 13 x 9-inch baking pan with waxed paper; set aside. In a large saucepan, combine chocolate chips, sweetened condensed milk, and margarine. Cook over low heat, stirring until chocolate melts and mixture is smooth. In a large bowl, combine peanuts and marshmallows. Pour chocolate mixture into peanut mixture; mix well. Spread over bottom of prepared pan. Chill 2 hours before cutting into squares.

Sugar Plums

Makes about 4½ pounds

  3 pounds pitted dates, peeled figs, seeded raisins, currants, apricots, and prunes*
  ½ pound blanched walnuts or almonds
  ½ pound unsalted shelled pistachio nuts
  ½ pound crystallized ginger
    Grated peel of 2 oranges
  3 tablespoons brandy or lemon juice
    Powdered or granulated sugar

Coarsely chop fruits, nuts, ginger, and orange peel in a food processor or food grinder. Add

lemon juice just until mixture is sticky enough to hold its shape. Shape into 1-inch balls. Roll balls in sugar. Wrap each in plastic wrap.
*Vary fruit and nut combination according to individual taste.

White Fudge

Makes about 1½ pounds

  2 cups sugar
  ½ cup dairy sour cream
  ⅓ cup white corn syrup
  2 tablespoons butter
  ¼ teaspoon salt
  2 teaspoons vanilla
  ¼ cup quartered candied cherries
  1 cup chopped walnuts

In a heavy 2-quart saucepan, combine sugar, sour cream, corn syrup, butter, and salt. Bring to boiling over medium heat, stirring constantly. Boil without stirring until the mixture reaches 236° F. on a candy thermometer. Remove from heat; let stand 15 minutes without stirring. Butter an 8-inch square pan; set aside. Stir vanilla into candy mixture. Beat with an electric mixer until mixture begins to lose its glossiness. Quickly stir in candied cherries and nuts. Pour into prepared pan. Let stand until cool. Cut into pieces.

Peanut Butter Fudge

Makes about 1½ pounds

  ½ cup unsweetened cocoa
  3 cups sugar
  ⅛ teaspoon salt
  1 cup milk
  3 tablespoons light corn syrup
  2 tablespoons butter
  1 cup crunchy peanut butter, warmed

In a small bowl, combine cocoa, sugar, and salt; set aside. In a heavy, 2-quart saucepan, combine milk and corn syrup. Carefully stir in sugar mixture. Cook over medium heat until sugar dissolves, stirring constantly and scraping sides of pan. Cook without stirring until mixture reaches 236° F. on a candy thermometer. Remove from heat. Add butter but do not stir. Let stand until 110° F. Butter an 8-inch square baking pan; set aside. Beat fudge with an electric mixer until candy begins to thicken. Quickly stir in peanut butter. Stir until mixture begins to lose its glossiness. Pour into prepared pan. Let stand until cool. Cut into pieces.

White Fudge, this page

Ice Cream and Frozen Desserts

Cranberry Raspberry Ice Cream

Makes about 1 quart

> 1 cup milk
> ⅓ cup sugar
> ¼ teaspoon salt
> 1 egg
> 1 can (16 ounces) cranberry raspberry sauce
> 1 cup half-and-half
> ½ teaspoon vanilla

In a small saucepan, heat milk. Add sugar and salt; stir until dissolved. In a small bowl, beat the egg. Stir a small amount of milk mixture into the beaten egg; return all to milk mixture. Cook over low heat, stirring constantly for 5 minutes. Refrigerate until well chilled. In a large bowl, break up cranberry raspberry sauce with a fork. Stir in egg mixture, half-and-half, and vanilla. Pour into a 2-quart metal ice cream freezer container. Churn and freeze according to manufacturer's directions.

Note: To make without a freezer, follow above instructions, except pour mixture into freezer trays and place in freezer for 2 hours. Transfer to a chilled bowl; beat well. Cover and return to freezer. Repeat beating after 2 hours; cover and return to freezer.

Peach Sherbet

Makes 12 servings

> 1 cup sugar
> 2½ cups water
> 2½ cups crushed fresh peaches
> 3 tablespoons sugar
> 1 can (6 ounces) frozen orange juice concentrate, thawed
> ¼ cup lemon juice
> 2 egg whites
> ¼ cup sugar
> 1 cup whipping cream, whipped

In a medium saucepan, combine 1 cup sugar and water. Bring to boiling; simmer 5 minutes. In a bowl, combine peaches, 3 tablespoons sugar, orange juice, and lemon juice. Stir in sugar-water mixture; blend well. Pour into a freezer tray.

Freeze until partially frozen, stirring occasionally. In a small bowl, beat egg whites until foamy. Gradually add remaining ¼ cup sugar, beating until stiff peaks form. Transfer frozen mixture to a bowl; beat until smooth. Fold in egg whites and whipped cream. Return to freezer until firm.

Strawberry Ice Cream

Makes about 2 quarts

> 1 quart fresh strawberries, mashed *or* 2 packages (16 ounces each) frozen whole unsweetened strawberries, thawed and mashed
> 1½ cups sugar
> 2 cans (13 ounces each) evaporated milk
> 1 tablespoon lemon juice

In a bowl, combine strawberries and sugar. Stir in evaporated milk and lemon juice. Refrigerate until well chilled. Pour into a 2-quart ice cream freezer container. Churn and freeze according to manufacturer's directions.

Note: To make without a freezer, pour milk into a large mixing bowl. Freeze until ice crystals form on outside edge. Remove from freezer; beat until foamy. Stir in ¾ cup sugar, 1 pint mashed fresh strawberries, and 2 teaspoons lemon juice. Beat until doubled in volume. Pour into a 9-inch square baking pan. Freeze until firm.

Peach Ice Cream

Makes 2 quarts

> 2 cups milk
> 1 cup whipping cream
> 1¼ cups powdered sugar
> Pinch salt
> 1½ teaspoons vanilla
> 1 cup mashed ripe peaches
> 3 egg whites, beaten until stiff

In a large bowl, beat milk, whipping cream, sugar, salt, and vanilla until smooth. Pour into a 2-quart ice cream freezer container. Churn and freeze according to manufacturer's directions, adding peaches and egg whites after 8 minutes.

Grapefruit Sherbet

Makes about 1½ quarts

- 1 package (3 ounces) lemon-flavored gelatin
- 1 cup boiling water
- 4 cups grapefruit juice
  Creme de menthe

In a bowl, dissolve gelatin in boiling water. Stir in grapefruit juice. Transfer to a 1½-quart container. Cover and freeze until partially frozen, stirring occasionally. Transfer to a bowl; beat until smooth. Return to freezer until firm. Serve in dessert dishes topped with creme de menthe.

Berry Blender Ice Cream

Makes 4 to 5 servings

- ½ cup whipping cream
- 2 eggs
- ⅓ cup sugar
- 3 cups whole frozen strawberries
- 2 teaspoons lemon juice

In a blender or food processor, blend whipping cream, eggs, and sugar. With machine running, drop in berries, one at a time; blend until smooth. Stir in lemon juice. Spoon into serving dishes. Serve immediately or place in freezer and remove 15 to 20 minutes before serving time.

Butter Pecan Pumpkin Ice Cream Pie

Makes 6 to 8 servings

- 1½ cups crushed gingersnap cookies
- ¼ cup butter *or* margarine, melted
- 1 cup canned pumpkin
- ¼ cup packed brown sugar
- 1 teaspoon ground cinnamon
- ¾ teaspoon ground nutmeg
- ½ teaspoon ground ginger
- ½ teaspoon ground cloves
- 1 quart butter pecan ice cream, slightly softened
  Whipped cream, optional

In a 9-inch pie pan, mix gingersnap crumbs and melted butter. Press firmly onto bottom and side of pan. Bake at 350° F. for 5 to 7 minutes. Set the crust aside to cool. In a small saucepan, combine pumpkin, brown sugar, and spices. Cook over low heat, stirring occasionally until heated through. Let stand until cool, then blend thoroughly with the ice cream. Pour into crust. Freeze for 4 hours or until firm. Garnish with whipped cream, if desired.

Baked Alaska Tarts

Makes 4 servings

- 3 tablespoons currant jelly
- 4 baked tart shells
- 1 pint vanilla ice cream
- 2 egg whites
- 3 tablespoons sugar
  Dash salt
- ¼ teaspoon vanilla

Spread jelly on bottoms of tart shells. Place a scoop of ice cream in each tart shell. In a small bowl, beat egg whites until foamy. Gradually beat in sugar, salt, and vanilla until stiff peaks form a meringue. Spread meringue over ice cream. Place tart shells on a cutting board. Bake at 450° F. for about 3 minutes or until delicately browned. Serve immediately.

Any-Berry Topping

Makes about 2 cups

- 1 can (16 to 17 ounces) blackberries, boysenberries, marionberries, blueberries, *or* raspberries
- 1 tablespoon cornstarch
- 1 of the following flavorings:
  1 tablespoon lemon juice, fruit-flavored liqueur *or* brandy; ½ teaspoon cinnamon *or* nutmeg; ½ teaspoon grated lemon *or* orange peel
- 1 to 2 tablespoons butter, optional

Drain berries; reserve syrup. In a small saucepan, combine reserved syrup and cornstarch; stir to dissolve cornstarch. Cook and stir until thickened. Add desired flavoring and butter, if desired. Gently stir in berries. Serve over ice cream, pound cake, or angel food cake.

Lemon Medley Sauce

Makes 3 cups

- 2 teaspoons grated lemon peel
- ½ cup lemon juice
- 2 cups sugar
- ¾ cup butter
- 4 eggs, lightly beaten

In a small saucepan, combine lemon peel and juice, sugar, and butter. Cook over low heat, stirring constantly until sugar dissolves. Stir a small amount of the hot mixture into eggs. Return all to the saucepan. Cook over medium heat, stirring constantly until mixture thickens slightly. Do not boil. Let stand until cool. Serve over ice cream or pound cake.

Cherries Jubilee Pie

Makes 8 to 10 servings

> 1 baked 9-inch piecrust (recipe on page 15)
> 1 pint vanilla ice cream
> 2 cans (16½ ounces each) pitted dark sweet cherries
> 3 tablespoons cornstarch
> 1 teaspoon grated orange peel
> ¼ cup brandy
>   Meringue (recipe follows)

Place piecrust in freezer to chill thoroughly. Soften ice cream slightly; spread evenly in piecrust. Cover with plastic wrap and freeze overnight. Place cherries in refrigerator to chill. The next day, drain cherries, reserving syrup. Refrigerate the cherries. In a saucepan, combine reserved syrup and cornstarch. Cook over medium heat, stirring constantly until thickened. Stir in orange peel and brandy. Let stand until cool. Press a piece of plastic wrap directly onto surface of the sauce. Refrigerate until well chilled. Prepare Meringue. Preheat oven to 475° F. Working quickly, remove filled piecrust from freezer. Spoon chilled cherries on top. Spoon ½ to ¾ cup chilled cherry sauce over cherries. Spread Meringue over the top, being certain to seal edge of crust. Bake for 1½ to 2 minutes or until meringue is lightly browned.

Meringue

> 3 egg whites
> ½ teaspoon vanilla
> ¼ teaspoon cream of tartar
> ¼ teaspoon salt
> ⅓ cup sugar

In a small bowl, beat egg whites until foamy. Gradually beat in vanilla, cream of tartar, and salt until soft peaks form. Gradually add sugar, beating until stiff peaks form.

Cookie Marlow

Makes 8 servings

> 3 cups diced rhubarb
> ¼ cup water
> ½ cup sugar
> 1½ cups quartered large marshmallows
> 1 cup whipping cream, whipped
> 2 cups coarsely broken crisp chocolate wafer cookies

In a saucepan, combine rhubarb and water; cook until just tender. Stir in sugar and marshmallows until well blended. Refrigerate until slightly thickened. Fold rhubarb mixture and broken cookies into whipped cream. Transfer to a freezer tray. Freeze until firm.

Rum Tortoni

Makes 6 servings

> 1 tablespoon butter
> 2 tablespoons chopped almonds
> ¼ teaspoon almond extract
> ½ cup vanilla wafer crumbs (about 16 cookies)
> 2 tablespoons powdered sugar
> 2 tablespoons light rum
> 1 cup whipping cream, whipped
> 3 maraschino cherries, halved and drained

In a small saucepan, melt butter. Sauté almonds until golden. Remove from heat. Stir in almond extract and all but 2 tablespoons of the cooky crumbs. Stir sugar and rum into the whipped cream, then fold in crumb mixture. Line a muffin pan with 6 paper baking cups. Spoon tortoni mixture into cups. Sprinkle with reserved crumbs. Top each with a cherry half. Freeze until firm. Cover and let stand at room temperature to soften slightly before serving.

Strawberry Cheese Parfait

Makes 6 servings

> 1 carton (8 ounces) cream-style cottage cheese, sieved
> 1 cup whipping cream, whipped
> ½ teaspoon salt
> 1 teaspoon vanilla
> 2 tablespoons sugar
> 1 egg white
> 1½ cups fresh *or* frozen strawberries

In a bowl, combine cottage cheese, whipped cream, salt, vanilla, and sugar; blend well. In a small bowl, beat egg white until soft peaks form. Fold egg white into cottage cheese mixture. In parfait glasses, alternate spoonfuls of cheese mixture with strawberries. Freeze until firm. Remove from freezer 20 minutes before serving.

Sherbet and Ladyfinger Loaf

Makes 10 to 12 servings

> 1 pint orange sherbet, slightly softened
> 1 package (3 ounces) ladyfingers
> 1 pint raspberry sherbet, slightly softened
> 2 cups frozen nondairy whipped topping, thawed
> 1 cup multicolored miniature marshmallows

Spread orange sherbet in the bottom of a 9 x 5-inch loaf pan. Arrange twelve double ladyfingers crosswise over sherbet. Spread raspberry sherbet over ladyfingers. Place in freezer until almost solid. Stir marshmallows into topping; spread over raspberry sherbet. Return to freezer until firm. To unmold, dip pan in hot water. Loosen edge with a spatula. Invert onto a serving platter.

Sherbet and Ladyfinger Loaf, this page

Fruit Desserts

Sunday Supper Pears

Makes 3 servings

3 fresh Anjou, Bosc, or Comice pears
½ cup chopped dates
¼ cup chopped walnuts
¼ cup butter
¼ cup honey
Nutmeg
½ cup sauterne or orange juice
Rum Custard Sauce (recipe follows)

Preheat oven to 350° F. Halve and core the pears. In a bowl, combine dates and nuts; spoon into centers of the pears. Place the pears in a baking dish; dot with butter, drizzle with honey, and sprinkle with nutmeg. Pour sauterne into the baking dish. Cover and bake 30 to 40 minutes or until pears are tender. Serve with Rum Custard Sauce.

Rum Custard Sauce

Makes about 1 cup

1 cup milk
2 egg yolks, lightly beaten
2 tablespoons sugar
Dash salt
1 teaspoon rum extract

In a saucepan, combine all ingredients; cook over low heat until thickened, stirring constantly.

Fresh Fruit Compote in a Pumpkin Shell

Makes 8 to 10 servings

⅔ cup orange juice
⅓ cup lemon juice
⅓ cup packed brown sugar
1 cinnamon stick
½ teaspoon grated orange peel
½ teaspoon grated lemon peel
3 apples peeled, cored, and cubed
2 pears, cored and cubed
1 banana, peeled and sliced
1 papaya, halved and seeded
1 medium pumpkin

In a medium saucepan, combine orange juice, lemon juice, brown sugar, cinnamon stick, and orange and lemon peel. Bring to boiling; reduce heat. Simmer 5 minutes. In a large bowl, combine apples, pears, and banana. Scoop out pulp from papaya halves with a melon ball cutter. Add papaya balls to the bowl of cut-up fruit. Pour hot syrup over fruit. Cover and refrigerate 1 to 2 hours. Remove cinnamon stick. Cut top off pumpkin; remove seeds and stringy portion. Fill pumpkin with fruit mixture and serve.

Fried Bananas

Makes 4 to 5 servings

1¼ cups all-purpose flour
1 jumbo egg
1 cup milk
¼ teaspoon salt
8 large bananas, peeled and cut in half lengthwise, then cut into 3-inch pieces
¼ cup light rum
½ cup granulated sugar
¾ teaspoon cinnamon
2 cups vegetable oil
½ cup powdered sugar

In a mixing bowl, combine flour, egg, milk, and salt. Let batter stand for 20 minutes. Place bananas in a glass dish; pour rum over all. Combine sugar and cinnamon; sprinkle over bananas. In a large skillet, heat oil to 365° F. Dip bananas in batter. Fry 6 at a time, turning to brown both sides. Drain on paper towels. Sprinkle bananas with powdered sugar.

Peach Haystacks

Makes 6 servings

1 can (16 ounces) peach halves, drained thoroughly
¼ cup crushed shredded wheat
2 tablespoons butter or margarine, melted
2 tablespoons brown sugar
2 tablespoons flaked coconut
2 tablespoons chopped pecans
¼ teaspoon ground cinnamon

Place peach halves on paper towels to absorb excess moisture. Place peach halves, hollow sides up, in an 11 x 8-inch baking dish; set aside. In a small bowl, combine shredded wheat, butter, brown sugar, coconut, pecans, and cinnamon; blend well. Spoon wheat mixture into centers of peaches. Broil for 3 minutes or until lightly toasted.

Fresh Fruit Parfait

Makes 4 servings

  1 cup sour cream
  1 tablespoon grated orange peel
  1 tablespoon honey
  1 tablespoon brown sugar
  1 orange, peeled and cut into bite-size pieces
  1 banana, sliced
  1 apple, cut into bite-size pieces
  ½ cup pineapple chunks

In a small bowl, combine sour cream, orange peel, honey, and brown sugar. Layer fruit with yogurt mixture in 4 parfait glasses or serving dishes.

Stuffed Cinnamon Apples

Makes 6 servings

  5 medium apples
  ⅔ cup red cinnamon candies
  3 cups water
  1 package (3 ounces) cream cheese, softened
  2 tablespoons milk
  1 teaspoon lemon juice
  ⅓ cup chopped dates
  1 can (8 ounces) crushed pineapple, drained
  2 tablespoons chopped walnuts

Peel and core apples. In a large saucepan, combine cinnamon candies and water. Cook over low heat until the candies are dissolved, stirring often. Place the apples upright in the saucepan. Simmer, uncovered, about 15 minutes or until the apples are tender. Allow to cool to room temperature, then refrigerate overnight. In a mixing bowl, combine cream cheese, milk, and lemon juice; beat until smooth. Add dates, pineapple, and nuts; blend well. Drain cooking liquid from apples. Stuff centers with cream cheese mixture.

Sweet Cherry Fruit Cup

Makes 4 to 6 servings

  1 can (16 ounces) pitted red cherries, drained; reserve ¾ cup liquid
  2 whole allspice
  2 whole cloves
  1 cinnamon stick
  1 Golden Delicious apple, cored and cubed
  1 tablespoon lemon juice
  1 orange, peeled and sliced
  ¾ cup sparkling cider *or* club soda
  3 to 4 drops red food coloring, optional
  Mint sprigs, optional

In a saucepan, combine reserved cherry syrup and spices. Bring to boiling; reduce heat. Cover and simmer 20 minutes. Let stand until cool; strain syrup. In a medium bowl, toss apple with lemon juice to prevent discoloration. Cut orange slices into half-rounds. Add orange and cherries to apple. Pour cooled syrup over fruit. Refrigerate 3 to 4 hours. Stir in cider and food coloring. Garnish with mint sprigs, and serve immediately.

Pears Melba

Makes 6 servings

  2 cans (29 ounces each) pear halves, drained; reserve syrup
  1 package (3 ounces) cream cheese, softened
  1 tablespoon powdered sugar
  ¼ cup chopped nuts
  1 tablespoon cornstarch
  ¼ cup water
  1 package (10 ounces) frozen raspberries, thawed
  ¼ cup brandy

Place 12 pear halves, cut sides down, on paper towels to absorb excess moisture. In a small bowl, combine cream cheese, sugar, and reserved pear syrup; blend well. Stir in nuts. Spread about 1 tablespoon cream cheese mixture over flat sides of pears. Press 2 halves together to make a whole pear. Repeat for remaining halves. Place pears in a serving dish; set aside. In a small saucepan, dissolve cornstarch in water. Stir in berries. Cook over medium heat, stirring constantly until thickened. Strain to remove seeds. Return berry mixture to pan; keep warm over low heat. Heat the brandy; pour over raspberry sauce. Ignite and immediately pour the flaming sauce over pears. Serve in individual dishes topped with sauce.

Chocolate Dipped Grapes

Makes about 30 grape clusters

  ½ to ¾ pound seedless grapes
  3 squares (1 ounce each) semisweet baking chocolate
  1 teaspoon vegetable shortening

Wash grapes and dry thoroughly; chill. Divide into clusters of 2 or 3 grapes. In the top of a double boiler, melt chocolate and shortening over simmering water. Dip each cluster into the chocolate to coat half of each grape. Place in small paper cups and chill until chocolate sets. Remove from refrigerator 15 minutes before serving. Use as a garnish on cakes or ice cream desserts.

Puddings, Soufflés, Mousses, and Meringues

Strawberry Mousse with Raspberry Sauce

Makes 8 to 10 servings

4½ cups sliced strawberries
1⅓ cups sugar
1½ tablespoons cornstarch
2 tablespoons unflavored gelatin
⅓ cup kirsch
2 cups whipping cream
Raspberry Sauce (recipe follows)

Lightly oil a 2-quart mold; set aside. In a large saucepan, combine strawberries and 1 cup of the sugar. Bring to boiling, then cook over low heat, stirring constantly until sugar dissolves. Chill just until syrupy but not firm. Stir cornstarch and gelatin into kirsch; let stand 5 minutes. In a small bowl, gradually add the remaining ⅓ cup sugar to the whipping cream, beating until stiff. Fold whipped cream into the strawberry mixture, then pour into the prepared mold. Refrigerate 8 hours. Unmold mousse onto a serving plate. Serve with Raspberry Sauce.

Raspberry Sauce

1 pint strawberries, sliced
1 package (10 ounces) frozen raspberries, thawed
¼ cup kirsch
2 tablespoons sugar
1 teaspoon grated orange peel

Thoroughly mix all ingredients. Let stand ½ hour to blend flavors.

Lemon Cooler Soufflé

Makes 8 servings

2 envelopes unflavored gelatin
½ cup water
6 eggs
1½ cups sugar
2 cups whipping cream, divided
1 tablespoon grated lemon peel
⅓ cup lemon juice
Lemon slices, optional
Whipped cream, optional

Cut a sheet of aluminum foil long enough to fit around the side of a 4-cup soufflé dish; fold lengthwise in half. Fasten to the dish to make a collar that stands 2 inches above the rim. In a small saucepan, sprinkle gelatin over the water, and let stand 5 minutes. Cook over very low heat, stirring constantly until gelatin dissolves. Remove from heat; let stand until cool. In a large bowl, beat eggs and sugar until thickened and light-colored. In a separate bowl, beat 1½ cups whipping cream until stiff; refrigerate. Stir lemon peel and juice into cooled gelatin. Pour into the egg mixture; beat at low speed until well blended. Fold in whipped cream. Pour into prepared dish. Refrigerate at least 3 hours or until set. Gently remove the collar. Whip remaining ½ cup cream. Garnish soufflé with whipped cream and lemon slices, if desired.

Baked Custard with Blackberry Sauce

Makes 6 servings

3 eggs
⅓ cup sugar
Salt
2½ cups milk, scalded
½ teaspoon vanilla
¾ teaspoon grated lemon peel, divided
1 can (17 ounces) blackberries
2 teaspoons cornstarch
1 teaspoon brandy, optional

Preheat oven to 350° F. In a bowl, combine eggs, sugar, and ¼ teaspoon salt; beat until light-colored. Gradually blend in milk, vanilla, and ½ teaspoon lemon peel. Pour into six 6-ounce custard cups. Place cups in a 13 x 9-inch baking dish. Fill with ½ inch hot water. Bake for 35 to 40 minutes or until a knife inserted near the center comes out clean. Cool to room temperature. Refrigerate until chilled. Drain the blackberries, reserving syrup. In a saucepan, combine cornstarch, remaining ¼ teaspoon lemon peel, and a dash of salt. Gradually add the reserved syrup; blend until smooth. Cook over medium heat, stirring constantly until thickened. Stir in brandy. Allow the sauce to cool, then stir in the blackberries. Refrigerate until chilled. Unmold custard into serving dishes. Top with blackberry sauce.

Carolina Dessert Whip

Makes 4 servings

²/₃ cup mashed cooked yams, chilled
½ teaspoon grated orange peel
⅓ cup orange juice
3 tablespoons sugar
2 teaspoons molasses
1 teaspoon lemon juice
2 egg whites
¼ teaspoon cream of tartar
    Dash salt
    Toasted coconut
    Sweetened whipped cream

In a bowl, mix yams, orange peel and juice, sugar, molasses, and lemon juice until well blended. In a small bowl, beat egg whites with cream of tartar and salt until stiff peaks form. Fold egg whites into yam mixture. Spoon into serving dishes. Sprinkle with toasted coconut. Garnish with whipped cream, if desired.

Vanilla Pudding with Sweet Cherry Sauce

Makes 6 servings

5 tablespoons cornstarch
⅓ cup sugar
¼ teaspoon salt
1 cup milk
2 cups half-and-half
1 teaspoon vanilla
½ teaspoon almond extract
    Sweet Cherry Sauce (recipe follows)

In the top of a double boiler, combine cornstarch, sugar, and salt. Gradually blend in milk and half-and-half. Cook over boiling water 10 minutes or until thickened and smooth, stirring constantly. Cover and cook 15 minutes, stirring occasionally. Add vanilla and almond extracts; beat until creamy. Pour into a 1-quart mold or six 6-ounce custard cups. Chill until firm. Unmold onto a serving plate or individual serving dishes. Serve with Sweet Cherry Sauce.

Sweet Cherry Sauce

1 can (16 ounces) pitted dark *or* light sweet cherries, drained; reserve syrup
2 teaspoons cornstarch
¼ cup red currant jelly

In a saucepan, combine reserved cherry syrup, cornstarch, and jelly. Cook over low heat, stirring constantly until thickened and smooth. Stir in cherries. Let stand until cool.

Chocolate Mousse

Makes 6 servings

4 squares (1 ounce each) semisweet chocolate
4 eggs, separated
¼ cup butter
2 tablespoons Grand Marnier *or* 1 teaspoon vanilla
¼ cup sugar
    Sweetened whipped cream
    Crisp vanilla cookies, optional

Place chocolate in a medium saucepan and cover with about 2 inches hot water. Cover the pan and let the chocolate stand about 5 minutes. The chocolate should be soft when tested with a fork. Carefully pour off the water. (Some water may cling to the chocolate.) Stir in egg yolks, one at a time, using a wire whisk. Cook over low heat, stirring constantly until thickened. Remove from heat. Blend in butter, one tablespoon at a time. Stir in liqueur. Cool slightly. In a mixing bowl, beat egg whites until foamy. Add sugar, one tablespoon at a time, beating until stiff peaks form. Pour chocolate mixture into a large mixing bowl; fold in about ¼ of the egg whites with a wire whisk. Use a rubber spatula to fold in remaining egg whites. Pour into a glass serving bowl or individual serving dishes. Chill about 1 hour before serving. Garnish with whipped cream and serve with crisp vanilla cookies, if desired.

Chocolate Soufflé

Makes 6 servings

4 eggs, separated
3 tablespoons butter
3 tablespoons flour
1 cup milk
²/₃ cup sugar, divided
2 squares (1 ounce each) semisweet chocolate
1½ teaspoons vanilla
¼ teaspoon salt

Preheat oven to 325° F. In a bowl, lightly beat the egg yolks; set aside. In a small saucepan, melt the butter. Stir in flour; cook and stir until bubbly. Gradually add milk and ⅓ cup of the sugar, stirring constantly until thickened. Add the chocolate; stir until melted. Add the chocolate mixture to egg yolks; stir in vanilla. In a small bowl, beat egg whites and salt until foamy. Gradually add the remaining ⅓ cup sugar, beating until stiff peaks form. Fold chocolate mixture into the egg whites. Turn into a 1½-quart casserole. Bake 60 to 75 minutes or until a knife inserted between center and outside edge comes out clean.

Frozen Daiquiri Soufflé

Makes 12 servings

8 eggs, separated
2 cups sugar, divided
Pinch salt
½ cup lime juice
½ cup lemon juice
Grated peel of 2 lemons
Grated peel of 2 limes
2 tablespoons unflavored gelatin
½ cup light rum
2 cups whipping cream
Yellow and green food coloring
Crushed pistachio nuts

In a large saucepan, beat the egg yolks until light-colored. Gradually add 1 cup of the sugar, beating until smooth and thickened. Blend in salt and juice and peel of limes and lemons. Cook over low heat, stirring constantly until thickened. Sprinkle the gelatin over the rum; let it stand 5 minutes to soften. Add gelatin to the custard; stir until gelatin dissolves. Allow to cool. Tint the custard with 2 drops of green and 1 drop of yellow food coloring. In a large bowl, beat egg whites until foamy. Gradually add remaining 1 cup sugar, beating until stiff peaks form. In a separate bowl, beat whipping cream until stiff. Fold egg whites into custard. Fold in whipped cream. Pour into a 12-cup soufflé dish. Place the soufflé in the freezer until firm. Garnish with pistachios.

Fresh Peach Pudding

Makes 9 servings

⅔ cup sugar
⅓ cup water
9 ripe peaches, peeled, halved, and stoned
¼ cup butter *or* margarine
½ cup sugar
1 egg
½ cup milk
1½ cups flour
2½ teaspoons baking powder
Dash nutmeg
Foamy Custard Sauce (recipe follows)

Butter a 1½-quart shallow baking dish; set aside. In a saucepan, combine ⅔ cup sugar and water. Cook over low heat, stirring constantly, until the sugar dissolves. Simmer peach halves until tender. Remove from heat; set aside. Preheat oven to 375° F. In a bowl, cream butter and ½ cup sugar until well blended. Add the egg; beat until light and fluffy. Stir together flour, baking powder, and nutmeg. Add flour mixture alternately with milk to creamed mixture; blend well. Arrange peaches in prepared pan. Pour syrup over peaches. Pour batter on top. Bake for 30 minutes or until center is firm. Serve with Foamy Custard Sauce.

Foamy Custard Sauce

¼ cup butter
1 cup sugar
2 eggs, separated
½ cup milk
1 tablespoon lemon juice
½ teaspoon vanilla

In a bowl, cream butter, sugar, and egg yolks until light and fluffy. Blend in milk. Transfer the mixture to a saucepan. Place the saucepan in a larger pan filled with hot water. Cook, stirring often, until thickened. Stir in lemon juice and vanilla. Remove from heat. In a small bowl, beat egg whites until stiff peaks form. Fold egg whites into custard. Serve immediately.

Grape Bavarian Cloud

Makes 4 or 5 servings

3 eggs, separated
¼ cup sugar
¼ cup lemon juice
1 teaspoon grated lemon peel
Dash salt
1½ teaspoons unflavored gelatin
2 tablespoons orange liqueur *or* orange juice
½ cup whipping cream, whipped
1 cup grapes, halved and seeded, if necessary
2 tablespoons toasted sliced almonds
4 small grape clusters

In a small saucepan, beat egg yolks until light-colored. Gradually add sugar, beating until smooth. Add lemon juice, lemon peel, and salt; blend well. Cook over low heat, stirring constantly until the mixture thickens. Sprinkle gelatin over liqueur and let stand 5 minutes. Add the softened gelatin to the egg mixture; stir until dissolved. Allow to cool. In a small bowl, beat the egg whites until stiff peaks form. Gently fold egg whites and whipped cream into the egg yolk mixture. Fold in grapes. Spoon into individual dessert dishes. Chill at least 3 hours. Garnish with almonds and grape clusters.

Meringue Swirls with Orange Filling

Makes 6 servings

    3 egg whites
    ¼ teaspoon cream of tartar
    ⅛ teaspoon salt
    ¾ cup sugar
        Orange Whip (recipe follows)
    6 thin orange slices, cut into sixths

Line a large baking sheet with heavy brown paper or aluminum foil; set aside. Preheat oven to 275° F. In a small bowl, beat egg whites until foamy. Add cream of tartar and salt; beat until stiff peaks form. Gradually add sugar, beating until very stiff. Use a pastry bag or a spoon to shape meringue into six 3-inch rounds. Make a depression in the centers of the meringues with a spoon. Bake for 1 hour. Allow to cool. Fill the baked meringues with Orange Whip. Chill at least 12 hours. Garnish with orange sections before serving.

Orange Filling

    3 egg yolks
    2 tablespoons sugar
    ⅛ teaspoon salt
    6 tablespoons frozen orange juice concentrate, thawed
    1½ teaspoons grated orange peel
    1 cup whipping cream, whipped

In the top of a double boiler, beat egg yolks until light-colored. Add sugar, salt, and orange juice concentrate; blend well. Cook over boiling water, stirring constantly until thickened. Remove from heat. Stir in orange peel. Refrigerate until chilled. Fold in whipped cream.

Date Soufflé with Orange Sauce

Makes 6 servings

    ½ cup pitted dates, finely chopped
    6 tablespoons flour
    ¼ cup butter, softened
    1 cup milk, scalded
    2 tablespoons grated orange peel
    3 eggs, separated
    3 tablespoons sugar
        Orange Sauce (recipe follows)

In a small saucepan, mix dates and flour. Stir in butter. Gradually stir in scalded milk. Place the saucepan in a larger pan filled with hot water. Cook about 5 minutes, stirring constantly. Stir in orange peel. Remove from heat. In a small bowl, beat the egg yolks until light-colored, gradually beating in the sugar. Slowly stir the hot date mixture into the egg yolk mixture. Set aside to cool.

Preheat oven to 325° F. In a small bowl, beat egg whites until stiff peaks form. Gently fold into the cooled date mixture. Turn into a 1-quart casserole. Place the casserole in a larger pan of of hot water. Bake for 1 hour or until a knife inserted between center and outside edge comes out clean. Serve with Orange Sauce.

Orange Sauce

    ¾ cup sugar
        Few grains salt
    1 tablespoon cornstarch
    1 cup orange juice
    2 tablespoons grated orange peel
    ⅓ cup half-and-half *or* whipping cream

In a small saucepan, mix sugar, salt, and cornstarch. Stir in orange juice and peel. Cook over medium heat, stirring constantly until thickened. Cover and cook over boiling water 10 minutes. Stir in half-and-half; heat through.

Cranberry Almond Ice Cream Meringues

Makes 10 servings

    4 egg whites
    ¼ teaspoon salt
    1 cup sugar
    1 teaspoon vanilla
        Ice Cream
        Cranberry Almond Sauce (recipe follows)

Grease two large baking sheets. Line with waxed paper and grease the waxed paper lightly; set aside. Preheat oven to 250° F. In a bowl, lightly beat egg whites and salt until soft peaks form. Add sugar, two tablespoons at a time, beating after each addition until sugar is incorporated. Add vanilla; beat until stiff peaks form. Use a spoon or pastry bag to form 3-inch mounds on the prepared baking sheets. Bake 1 hour 15 minutes. Turn off the oven and remove the baking sheets. Scoop out centers of the meringues, and return shells to the oven for about 30 minutes or until dry. Fill centers with ice cream and top with Cranberry Almond Sauce.

Cranberry Almond Sauce

    1 cup cranberry orange sauce
    2 tablespoons almond-flavored liqueur
    ½ teaspoon almond extract

In a small bowl, combine all ingredients; blend well.

Reduced Calorie Desserts

Chocolate Nut Brownies

Makes 16 servings; 110 calories per serving

> 1 square (1 ounce) unsweetened baking chocolate
> 1/3 cup margarine
> 2 tablespoons liquid sweetener
> 2 teaspoons vanilla
> 2 eggs, lightly beaten
> 1 cup sifted cake flour
> 1/2 teaspoon salt
> 1/2 teaspoon baking soda
> 3/4 cup chopped nuts

Lightly grease an 8-inch square baking pan. Preheat oven to 350° F. In a small saucepan, melt chocolate and margarine over low heat, stirring constantly. Remove from heat. Stir in liquid sweetener, vanilla, and eggs; blend well. Stir together flour, salt, and baking soda. Gradually blend dry ingredients into chocolate mixture. Stir in nuts. Pour into the prepared pan. Bake for 20 minutes. Cool in pan on a wire rack. Cut into bars.

Coconut Cranberry Cookies

Makes 60 cookies; 39 calories per cooky

> 3/4 cup granulated sugar substitute
> 1/2 cup margarine
> 1 teaspoon coconut flavoring
> 3 tablespoons skim milk
> 1 1/2 cups sifted flour
> 1/2 teaspoon baking powder
> 1/2 teaspoon salt
> 3/4 cup coarsely chopped cranberries, drained
> 1/2 cup shredded coconut

In a large bowl, cream sugar substitute, margarine, and coconut flavoring until smooth. Add milk; blend well. Stir together flour, baking powder, and salt. Gradually blend into creamed mixture. Stir in cranberries. Divide the dough in half. Shape each half into a 1 1/2-inch diameter roll. Roll in shredded coconut. Wrap in waxed paper or plastic wrap. Chill 8 hours. Preheat oven to 375° F. Cut dough into thin slices. Place on an ungreased baking sheet. Bake for 12 to 15 minutes or until golden. Remove from baking sheet to a wire rack to cool.

Cheesecake

Makes 12 servings; 224 calories per serving

> 1/2 cup graham cracker crumbs
> 3 packages (8 ounces each) Neufchatel cheese, softened
> 1/3 cup sugar
> Sugar substitute to equal 6 tablespoons sugar
> 1 1/2 tablespoons flour
> 3/4 teaspoon grated orange peel
> 1 teaspoon vanilla
> 3 eggs
> 1 egg yolk
> 2 tablespoons skim milk

Generously butter the bottom and side of an 8-inch springform pan. Firmly press graham cracker crumbs onto the bottom of the pan. Chill 1 hour. Preheat oven to 250° F. In an electric blender or food processor, combine cheese, sugar, sugar substitute, flour, orange peel, vanilla, eggs, egg yolk, and milk. Blend until smooth. Spoon cheese mixture into the prepared pan. Bake for 1 hour 10 minutes. Turn the oven off; open the door and let the cake cool in the oven to room temperature. Chill cheesecake at least 4 hours before serving.

Peanut Butter Cookies

Makes 32 cookies; 26 calories per cooky

> 2/3 cup sifted flour
> 1/2 teaspoon baking soda
> 1/2 teaspoon baking powder
> 1/4 teaspoon salt
> 6 tablespoons peanut butter
> 2 eggs
> 1/2 cup granulated sugar substitute

Lightly grease a large baking sheet. Preheat oven to 375° F. Stir together flour, baking soda, baking powder, and salt; set aside. In a large bowl, blend peanut butter and eggs; blend in the sugar substitute. Gradually add the dry ingredients, beating well after each addition. Drop by teaspoonfuls onto the prepared baking sheet. Press with tines of a fork to flatten. Bake for 10 to 12 minutes or until golden. Remove from baking sheet to a wire rack to cool.

Skinny Vanilla Ice Cream

Makes 8 servings; 71 calories per serving

  1 can (13 ounces) evaporated skim milk
1¼ teaspoons unflavored gelatin
  ¼ cup sugar
  ⅓ cup cold water
     Granulated sugar substitute to equal 16 teaspoons
     sugar
  4 teaspoons vanilla
  ½ teaspoon butter flavoring
  2 egg whites
  ¼ teaspoon salt

Pour evaporated skim milk into a deep bowl. Place bowl and beaters of an electric mixer in the freezer for 1 hour or until milk begins to freeze. In a small saucepan, combine gelatin and sugar. Stir in water; let stand 1 minute. Heat slowly, stirring constantly until gelatin and sugar dissolve. Stir in sugar substitute, vanilla, and butter flavoring. Let stand until cool. Beat frozen milk at high speed until it has the consistency of whipped cream. In a small bowl, beat egg whites and salt until stiff peaks form. Fold gelatin mixture and egg whites into the whipped milk until blended. Pour into a 9-inch square pan. Freeze until almost firm. Beat with an electric mixer until smooth. Return to the freezer for 30 minutes. Beat again. Freeze until firm. Soften slightly before serving.

Snow Topped Pears

Makes 6 servings; 84 calories per serving

  2 ripe Bartlett pears, peeled, cored, and chopped
  2 tablespoons lemon juice
1½ tablespoons cornstarch
  4 tablespoons sugar, divided
  3 tablespoons fresh orange juice
  2 egg whites

In a saucepan, combine pears, lemon juice, cornstarch, 3 tablespoons sugar, and orange juice. Cook over medium heat, stirring constantly until mixture comes to boiling and begins to thicken. Pour the sauce into an 8-inch round baking dish. Chill thoroughly. Preheat oven to 450° F. In a small bowl, beat the egg whites until foamy. Gradually beat in the remaining 1 tablespoon sugar until stiff peaks form a meringue. Spoon the meringue over the pear mixture and bake until the meringue is golden. Serve warm.

Low-Cal Cherry Cobbler

Makes 4 servings; 155 calories per serving

  1 can (16 ounces) water-packed cherries; drained;
     reserve juice
  1 teaspoon cornstarch
  ½ teaspoon lemon juice
  ¼ teaspoon liquid sweetener
  ⅛ teaspoon almond extract
  ½ cup sifted cake flour
  ¾ teaspoon baking powder
  ⅛ teaspoon salt
  1 tablespoon margarine
  2 tablespoons skim milk
  ½ teaspoon liquid sweetener
  2 tablespoons beaten egg

Place cherries in an 8-inch pie plate or shallow baking pan. Measure reserved cherry juice. Add water, if necessary, to measure ⅔ cup. In a saucepan, combine cherry juice, cornstarch, lemon juice, ¼ teaspoon liquid sweetener, and almond extract. Cook over low heat, stirring constantly until slightly thickened. Pour sauce over cherries. In a large bowl, stir together cake flour, baking powder, and salt. Cut in margarine with a pastry blender or two knives until mixture resembles fine crumbs. Combine milk, ½ teaspoon liquid sweetener, and egg; blend well. Stir into dry ingredients. Drop batter in 4 spoonfuls onto cherries. Bake at 425° F. for 25 to 30 minutes or until golden brown. Serve warm.

Chocolate Chiffon Creme

Makes 8 servings; 77 calories per serving

  ¼ cup unsweetened cocoa
  1 tablespoon unflavored gelatin
  3 eggs, separated
1½ cups skim milk
  ¾ cup granulated sugar substitute
  ⅛ teaspoon salt
  1 teaspoon vanilla
  ¼ teaspoon cream of tartar

In the top of a double boiler, combine cocoa and gelatin. Lightly beat egg yolks. Gradually add egg yolks, milk, sugar substitute, and salt to the cocoa mixture. Cook over boiling water, stirring constantly until gelatin dissolves and mixture is slightly thickened. Stir in vanilla. Chill until partially thickened. In a small bowl, beat egg whites and cream of tartar until stiff peaks form. Fold in the cocoa mixture. Pour into a 4-cup ring mold or individual molds. Chill until firm.

Dessert Breads

Babas au Rhum

Makes 8 servings

  1 package (¼ ounce) active dry yeast
  1 teaspoon sugar
  ¼ cup lukewarm water (110 to 115° F.)
  ¼ cup milk, scalded and cooled
  6 tablespoons butter, softened
  ¼ teaspoon salt
  ¼ cup sugar
  3 eggs
  2 cups flour
  ½ cup cake flour
    Rum Syrup (recipe follows)
    Apricot Glaze (recipe follows)
  8 candied cherries

Sprinkle yeast and 1 teaspoon sugar over the water; let stand 5 minutes to soften yeast. In a small saucepan, combine milk, butter, and salt. Cook over low heat until butter melts; cool to room temperature. In a large bowl, combine ¼ cup sugar and eggs; beat until light-colored. Gradually add flours; blend well. Butter 8 baba molds* or custard cups. Fill the molds half full with batter. Cover with buttered aluminum foil or a damp cloth. Place the molds in a warm, draft-free place 20 to 25 minutes or until dough rises to the tops. Preheat oven to 350° F. Place the molds on a baking sheet. Bake for 15 minutes or until golden brown. Turn the babas out of molds and stand on a wire rack to cool. Place the rack over a baking sheet. Slowly drizzle Rum Syrup over babas; let stand until syrup is absorbed. Glaze babas with warm Apricot Glaze. Garnish each with a candied cherry. Refrigerate until ready to serve.
*Available in gourmet cooking shops.

Rum Syrup

  3 cups water
  1½ cups sugar
  ⅓ cup dark rum

In a small saucepan, heat water and sugar, stirring constantly about 5 minutes or until syrup is clear. Remove from heat. Stir in the rum.

Apricot Glaze

  1 cup apricot jam
  2 tablespoons sugar
  3 tablespoons dark rum

In a small saucepan, combine jam and sugar. Cook over medium heat until mixture reaches 228° F. on a candy thermometer. Stir in the rum.

Cinnamon Pinwheel Crisps

Makes about 30 servings

  1 tablespoon active dry yeast
  ¼ cup lukewarm water (110 to 115° F.)
  3 cups flour
  ½ teaspoon salt
  2 tablespoons sugar
  1 cup butter *or* margarine
  ½ cup milk
  1 egg, lightly beaten
  3 tablespoons vegetable oil
  ½ cup packed brown sugar
  ½ cup granulated sugar
  2 tablespoons ground cinnamon

Sprinkle yeast over water; let stand 5 minutes to soften yeast. In a large bowl, combine flour, salt, and 2 tablespoons sugar. Cut in butter with a pastry blender or two knives until particles are the size of small peas. In a separate bowl, blend milk, egg, and oil. Stir in yeast. Add yeast mixture to dry ingredients, stirring with a fork just until all ingredients are moistened. Cover and chill 1 hour. Turn dough out onto a floured surface. Knead 4 or 5 times. Roll the dough into an 18 x 11-inch rectangle. Combine sugars and cinnamon. Sprinkle part of the sugar mixture over the dough. Tightly roll up the dough from the long side. Pinch edges to seal. Wrap in plastic wrap; chill 1 hour or until firm. Preheat oven to 400° F. Cut dough into ½-inch slices. Dip both sides of each slice in remaining sugar mixture. Roll each slice into a 5-inch circle. Sprinkle with more sugar mixture if the dough sticks. Place dough rounds on an ungreased baking sheet. Bake for about 12 minutes or until lightly browned. Remove to a wire rack to cool. Store in an airtight container.

Babas au Rhum, this page

Strawberry Bread with Strawberry Cream Spread

Makes 8 servings

 1 cup butter *or* margarine
 1 cup sugar
 ½ teaspoon almond extract
 2 eggs, separated
 2 cups flour
 1 teaspoon baking powder
 1 teaspoon baking soda
 1 teaspoon salt
 1 cup crushed fresh strawberries or 1 package
   (10 ounces) frozen strawberries, thawed and drained
   Strawberry Cream Spread (recipe follows)

Line a 9 x 5-inch loaf pan with greased waxed paper; set aside. Preheat oven to 325° F. In a large bowl, cream butter, sugar, and almond extract until light and fluffy. Add egg yolks, one at a time, beating well after each addition. Stir together flour, baking powder, baking soda, and salt. Add dry ingredients alternately with crushed strawberries to creamed mixture. In a small bowl, beat egg whites until stiff peaks form. Pour batter into the prepared pan. Bake for 50 to 60 minutes or until a wooden pick inserted in the center comes out clean. Cool in pan 10 minutes. Turn out onto a wire rack to cool completely. Carefully peel off waxed paper.

Strawberry Cream Spread

 1 package (3 ounces) cream cheese, softened
 2 tablespoons strawberry jelly or preserves

In a small bowl, blend all ingredients.

Lemon Tea Bread with Orange Spread

Makes 1 loaf

 ¼ cup butter *or* margarine
 ¾ cup sugar
 2 eggs, lightly beaten
 2 teaspoons grated lemon peel
 2 cups flour
 2½ teaspoons baking powder
 ½ teaspoon salt
 ¾ cup milk
 ¼ to ½ cup chopped nuts
 2 tablespoons sugar
 2 tablespoons lemon juice
   Orange Spread (recipe follows)

Grease and flour a 9 x 5-inch loaf pan. Preheat oven to 350° F. In a large bowl, cream butter and sugar until well blended. Add eggs and lemon peel; blend well. Stir together flour, baking powder, and salt. Add flour mixture alternately with milk to the creamed mixture, beating well after each addition. Stir in nuts. Pour into the prepared pan. Bake for 50 to 60 minutes or until a wooden pick inserted in the center comes out clean. Cool in pan 10 minutes. Combine sugar and lemon juice. Drizzle over bread; let stand until lemon mixture is absorbed. Turn out onto a wire rack to cool completely. Serve with Orange Spread.

Orange Spread

 1 package (3 ounces) cream cheese, softened
 1 tablespoon orange juice
 1 teaspoon grated orange peel

In a small bowl, blend all ingredients.

Cherry Nut Bread with Almond Butter

Makes 1 loaf

 ½ cup butter *or* margarine
 1 cup sugar
 2 eggs
 2 cups flour
 1 teaspoon baking powder
 ½ teaspoon salt
 1 jar (10 ounces) maraschino cherries, drained,
   reserve juice
 1 teaspoon vanilla
 ½ cup chopped nuts
   Almond Butter (recipe follows)

Grease a 9 x 5-inch loaf pan. Preheat oven to 350° F. In a large bowl, cream butter and sugar until well blended. Add eggs, one at a time, beating well after each addition. Stir together flour, baking powder, and salt. Measure cherry juice, adding water, if necessary, to equal ½ cup. Add dry ingredients alternately with cherry juice and vanilla to creamed mixture; blend well. Cut cherries in halves and stir into the batter. Stir in nuts. Pour batter into the prepared pan. Bake for 1 hour or until a wooden pick inserted in the center comes out clean. Cool in pan 10 minutes. Turn out onto a wire rack to cool completely.

Almond Butter

 ½ cup butter *or* margarine, softened
 1 tablespoon finely chopped almonds
 ½ teaspoon almond extract

In a small bowl, blend all ingredients.

Jiffy Desserts

Strawberry Daiquiri Cake

Makes 16 servings

- 1 package (18.5 ounces) strawberry cake mix
- 3 eggs
- 3 tablespoons lemon juice
- 2 teaspoons rum extract
- 1 cup sliced strawberries *or* 1 package (10 ounces) frozen strawberries, thawed
  Lemon Rum Sauce (recipe follows)

Grease and flour a 12-cup fluted tube pan or 10-inch tube pan. Preheat oven to 350° F. In a large bowl, combine cake mix, eggs, lemon juice, and rum extract. Beat on low speed just until moistened. Beat on high speed 2 minutes. Stir in strawberries. Pour into the prepared pan. Bake for 40 to 50 minutes or until a wooden pick inserted near the center comes out clean. Cool in pan 25 minutes. Invert onto a serving plate; let stand until cool. Spoon Lemon Rum Sauce over cake.

Lemon Rum Sauce

- ½ cup powdered sugar
- 1½ teaspoons lemon juice
- 1 teaspoon water
- ½ teaspoon rum extract

In a small bowl, combine all ingredients; blend well.

Ugly Duckling Pudding Cake

Makes 12 to 16 servings

- 1 package (18.5 ounces) yellow cake mix
- 1 package (3 ounces) instant lemon pudding mix
- 1 can (16 ounces) fruit cocktail
- 4 eggs
- 1 cup flaked coconut
- ¼ cup vegetable oil
- ½ cup packed brown sugar
- ½ cup chopped nuts
  Butter Glaze (recipe follows)

Grease and flour a 13 x 9-inch baking pan; set aside. Preheat oven to 325° F. In a large bowl, combine cake mix, pudding mix, fruit cocktail and syrup, eggs, coconut, and oil; beat just until moistened. Beat on medium speed 4 minutes. Pour into the prepared pan. Sprinkle with brown sugar and nuts. Bake for 45 minutes or until a wooden pick inserted in the center comes out clean. Cool in pan 15 minutes. Spoon hot Butter Glaze over cake. Serve warm or cold.

Butter Glaze

- ⅓ cup butter
- ⅓ cup half-and-half
- ⅓ cup sugar

In a saucepan, combine all ingredients. Bring to boiling; boil 2 minutes.

Toasty Pineapple Angel Delight

Makes 6 servings

- ½ cup butter *or* margarine, softened
- ½ cup packed brown sugar
  Dash ground cinnamon
- 1 angel food loaf cake, cut in 6 slices
- 6 canned pineapple rings, drained
- ¾ cup dairy sour cream
- 6 maraschino cherries

Combine butter, brown sugar, and cinnamon; blend well; set aside. Toast one side of cake slices under broiler until golden. Spread butter mixture generously on untoasted side of cake slices. Top each with a pineapple ring and some of the remaining butter. Broil 1 to 2 minutes or until golden. Serve topped with sour cream and maraschino cherries.

Angel Fluff Dessert

Makes 8 servings

- 1 carton (12 ounces) cream-style cottage cheese
- 1 package (3 ounces) orange-flavored gelatin
- 1 can (8 ounces) pineapple tidbits, drained
- 1 can (17 ounces) fruit cocktail, drained
- 1 package (3 ounces) whipped topping mix

In a bowl, combine cottage cheese and gelatin; blend well. Stir pineapple and fruit cocktail into cottage cheese mixture. Prepare whipped topping mix according to package directions. Fold whipped topping into fruit mixture. Refrigerate until chilled. Serve in individual serving dishes.

Apple Streusel Dessert

Makes 8 to 10 servings

    1 package (18.5 ounces) yellow cake mix
    3 eggs
    1 can (21 ounces) apple pie filling
    1/3 cup packed brown sugar
    1 tablespoon flour
    1 tablespoon butter *or* margarine
    1 teaspoon ground cinnamon
    1 cup chopped nuts

Lightly grease a 13 x 9-inch baking pan; set aside. Preheat oven to 350° F. In a large bowl, combine cake mix, eggs, and pie filling; beat until moistened. Continue to beat on medium speed 4 minutes. Pour into the prepared pan. Mix brown sugar, flour, butter, cinnamon, and nuts; sprinkle over the batter. Bake for 35 minutes. Cool slightly in the pan before cutting into squares.

Angel Food Cake with Raspberry Creme

Makes 10 to 12 servings

    1 envelope unflavored gelatin
    1 can (17 ounces) raspberries, drained; reserve syrup
    1 to 3 drops red food coloring, optional
    1 cup whipping cream
    1 angel food cake

In a saucepan, combine gelatin and reserved raspberry syrup. Cook over low heat, stirring constantly, until gelatin dissolves. Stir in food coloring, if desired. Chill syrup until partially set. In a small bowl, beat the whipping cream until almost stiff. Gradually beat in partially set syrup. Fold in raspberries. Slice the cake and serve topped with raspberry creme.

Grasshopper Cake

Makes 12 servings

    1 package (18.5 ounces) white cake with pudding mix
    6 tablespoons green creme de menthe, divided
    1 can (16 ounces) chocolate ice cream topping
    1 container (8 ounces) frozen nondairy whipped dessert topping, thawed

Prepare cake mix according to package directions adding 3 tablespoons of the creme de menthe. Bake as directed in a 10 x 8-inch baking pan. Cool in pan on a wire rack. Spread ice cream topping over cake. Blend remaining 3 tablespoons creme de menthe into whipped topping. Spread the whipped topping over cake. Refrigerate until chilled.

Cherry Chip Cake

Makes 12 servings

    1 cup chopped nuts
    1 package (18.5 ounces) cherry chip cake mix
    1 box (3 ounces) instant vanilla pudding mix
    4 eggs
    1/2 cup vegetable oil
    1 cup water
    Rum Glaze (recipe follows)

Grease a 10-inch tube pan. Sprinkle nuts over bottom; set aside. In a large bowl, combine cake mix, pudding mix, eggs, oil, and water; beat on low speed just until moistened. Beat on high speed 2 minutes. Pour the batter into the prepared pan. Bake 45 to 50 minutes or until a wooden pick inserted in the center comes out clean. Cool in pan 15 minutes. Turn out onto a serving plate. Spoon Rum Glaze over cake.

Rum Glaze

    1 cup sugar
    1/2 cup water
    1/4 cup light rum

In a saucepan, combine sugar and water. Bring to a boil; remove from heat. Let stand 10 minutes. Stir in rum.

Cheery Cherry Cobbler

Makes 6 to 8 servings

    2 cups sugar
    1 cup milk
    2 teaspoons baking powder
    Pinch salt
    1¾ cups flour
    2½ cups sweet pitted cherries, divided
    1 tablespoon butter, cut in pieces
    2 cups boiling water

Grease a 13 x 9-inch baking pan; set aside. Preheat oven to 350° F. In a large mixing bowl, combine 1 cup sugar, milk, baking powder, salt, flour, and 1 cup cherries; blend well. Pour batter into the prepared pan. Combine remaining 1 cup sugar, 1½ cups cherries, butter, and boiling water. Pour over batter. Bake, uncovered, for 1 hour. Serve warm.

Cheery Cherry Cobbler, this page

Quick Fruit Cocktail Cake

Makes 9 servings

1 cup flour
1 cup sugar
¼ teaspoon salt
1 teaspoon baking soda
1 egg, lightly beaten
1 cup fruit cocktail, undrained
½ cup packed brown sugar
½ cup chopped nuts

Grease and flour a 9-inch square baking pan; set aside. Preheat oven to 350° F. Stir together flour, sugar, salt, and baking soda. Add egg and fruit cocktail; mix just until all ingredients are moistened. Pour into the prepared pan. Sprinkle with brown sugar and nuts. Bake for 35 to 40 minutes or until golden.

Easy Cheese Slices

Makes 16 to 20 servings

1 package (18.5 ounces) yellow cake mix
½ cup butter *or* margarine, melted and cooled
2 eggs, lightly beaten
1 package (8 ounces) cream cheese, softened
2 cups powdered sugar
2 eggs, well beaten
1 teaspoon vanilla

Butter a 15 x 10-inch jelly-roll pan; set aside. Preheat oven to 350° F. In a large bowl, combine cake mix, butter, and 2 eggs; blend well. Pat dough into the prepared pan. In a bowl, combine cream cheese, powdered sugar, remaining 2 eggs, and vanilla; blend until smooth. Pour over crust. Bake for 30 to 35 minutes or until set.

Five-Step Cake

Makes 12 to 16 servings

1 can (20 ounces) crushed pineapple
1 can (21 ounces) cherry pie filling
1 package (18.5 ounces) yellow cake mix
1 cup margarine
½ cup chopped nuts
   Half-and-half

Preheat oven to 350° F. Spread pineapple over bottom of a 13 x 9-inch baking pan. Spread pie filling over pineapple. Sprinkle cake mix over pie filling. Sprinkle pieces of margarine over cake mix. Top with nuts. Bake for 1 hour. Cool slightly in pan. Cut into pieces and serve with half-and-half.

Harvey Wallbanger Cake

Makes 12 servings

1 package (18.5 ounces) orange-flavored cake mix
1 package (3 ounces) instant vanilla pudding mix
½ cup vegetable oil
4 eggs
¼ cup Galliano liqueur
¼ cup vodka
¾ cup orange juice
   Orange Glaze (recipe follows)

Grease a 10-inch tube pan; set aside. Preheat oven to 350° F. In a large bowl, combine cake mix, pudding mix, oil, and eggs. Beat on low speed just until blended. Add Galliano, vodka, and orange juice; blend well. Beat on high speed 2 minutes. Pour batter into the prepared pan. Bake for 45 to 55 minutes or until a wooden pick inserted near the center comes out clean. Cool in pan 15 minutes. Turn out onto a serving plate. Drizzle Orange Glaze over cake.

Orange Glaze

1½ tablespoons Galliano liqueur
1½ tablespoons vodka
1½ tablespoons orange juice
1 cup powdered sugar

In a small bowl, combine all ingredients; blend well.

Peach Tapioca Cream

Makes 4 servings

1 package (3¼ ounces) vanilla tapioca pudding mix
2 cups milk
1 can (16 ounces) sliced peaches, drained

Prepare tapioca according to package directions using 2 cups milk. Let stand to cool slightly. Layer peach slices and tapioca in 4 serving dishes. Serve at room temperature or chilled.

Pistachio Dessert

Makes 6 to 8 servings

1 can (20 ounces) crushed pineapple
1 package (3 ounces) pistachio pudding mix
1 cup miniature marshmallows
¼ cup finely chopped nuts
1 container (9 ounces) frozen nondairy whipped dessert topping, thawed

In a bowl, combine pineapple and juice and pudding mix; blend well. Stir in marshmallows and nuts. Fold in whipped topping. Refrigerate until chilled. Serve in individual dishes.

Chocolate Cherry Cheesecake

Makes 12 to 16 servings

- 1 package (9 ounces) chocolate cake mix
- 1 package (3 ounces) instant chocolate pudding mix
- 1 package (8 ounces) cream cheese, softened
- 1 can (21 ounces) cherry pie filling
  Whipped cream

Grease a 13 x 9-inch baking pan. Prepare cake mix and bake according to package directions. Cool in pan on a wire rack. Prepare pudding mix according to package directions. Add cream cheese to pudding; blend well. Spread the pudding mixture over cooled cake. Spread the cherry pie filling on top. Garnish with whipped cream. Refrigerate until chilled.

Cranberry Strawberry Shortcake

Makes 6 servings

- 1 can (8 ounces) whole berry cranberry sauce
- 1 package (10 ounces) frozen strawberries in syrup, thawed
- ½ teaspoon lemon juice
- 6 individual shortcakes
  Whipped cream

In a bowl, break up cranberry sauce with a fork. Stir in strawberries and lemon juice. Spoon sauce over shortcakes. Top with whipped cream.

Grape Almond Cream Cake

Makes 8 servings

- 1 can (16 ounces) green grapes, drained; reserve syrup
- 1 envelope unflavored gelatin
- 1 tablespoon sugar
- ¼ to ½ teaspoon almond extract
- 1 cup whipping cream, whipped
- 1 package (9 ounces) yellow cake mix, prepared according to package directions, adding ½ teaspoon almond extract to batter

In a saucepan, combine reserved syrup and gelatin. Cook over low heat, stirring constantly until gelatin dissolves. Combine gelatin mixture and grapes. Add water, if necessary, to equal 2 cups. Chill until partially set, stirring occasionally. Fold sugar and almond extract into whipped cream. Use a pastry bag or spoon to spread whipped cream along outside edge of cake to make a ¾-inch border. Spread the partially set grape mixture evenly inside whipped cream border on top of cake. Refrigerate until topping is firm. Garnish with remaining whipped cream.

Quick and Easy Cherry Dessert

Makes 12 to 16 servings

- 2 cans (21 ounces each) cherry pie filling
- 1 package (18.5 ounces) white cake mix
- ½ cup butter *or* margarine, melted
- 1 cup chopped nuts

Preheat oven to 375° F. Spread cherry pie filling evenly over the bottom of a 13 x 9-inch baking pan. Sprinkle cake mix evenly over cherries. Drizzle melted butter over cake mix. Sprinkle with nuts. Bake for 1 hour or until golden brown. Cool in pan slightly before cutting into squares.

Strawberry Angel Cake

Makes 12 servings

- 3 packages (3 ounces each) strawberry-flavored gelatin
- 3 cups boiling water
- 1 angel food cake, cut in 1-inch cubes
- 2 packages (16 ounces each) frozen strawberries in syrup, thawed
- 1½ cups whipping cream, whipped

Dissolve gelatin in boiling water; chill until partially set. Place angel food cake in a 13 x 9-inch baking pan. Spoon strawberries over cake. Spoon gelatin over berries. Refrigerate until gelatin is set. Spread whipped cream on top and serve.

Grape and Peach Shortcake

Makes 6 servings

- 1 can (29 ounces) sliced peaches, drained
- 1 cup grape halves, seeded, if necessary
- ⅓ cup sugar
- 1 teaspoon vanilla
- 6 individual shortcakes
  Whipped cream

In a small bowl, combine peaches, grapes, sugar, and vanilla; mix lightly. Refrigerate for at least 1 hour. Just before serving, slice each shortcake crosswise in half. Spoon about ¼ cup fruit on bottom half and top with other half. Spoon about ¼ cup fruit on top. Garnish with whipped cream.

Microwave Desserts

Graham Cracker Toffee Bars

Makes 24 servings

- 11 graham cracker squares
- ½ cup butter *or* margarine
- ½ cup packed brown sugar
- ½ cup powdered sugar
- 1 tablespoon cornstarch
- ¼ teaspoon salt
- 1 cup flaked coconut
- ½ cup chopped nuts
- 1 package (6 ounces) semisweet chocolate chips

In a 12 x 8-inch microsafe baking dish, arrange graham cracker squares in a single layer to cover the bottom. In a 1-quart microsafe casserole, combine butter and brown sugar. Microwave on High for 2 minutes; blend well. Stir in powdered sugar, cornstarch, salt, coconut, and nuts. Spread mixture evenly over graham crackers. Sprinkle chocolate chips on top. Microwave on High 2 minutes or until chocolate chips melt. Let cool slightly. Spread melted chocolate chips over the top. Cool before cutting into bars.

Delta Pecan Pie

Makes 8 servings

- 1 recipe Single Piecrust (page 15)
- ¼ cup butter *or* margarine
- 1 cup sugar
- ½ cup dark corn syrup
- 3 eggs, lightly beaten
- 1 teaspoon vanilla
- ⅛ teaspoon salt
- 1¼ cups pecan halves

Prepare piecrust dough. Roll out on a floured surface to 1 inch larger than an inverted 9-inch microsafe pie plate. Fit into pie plate, trim and flute edge, and prick bottom with a fork. Microwave on High 6 to 7 minutes or until dry and blistered; set aside. In a microsafe bowl, place butter. Microwave on High 1 minute or until butter melts. Stir in remaining ingredients, except whipped cream, in order; blend well. Pour into piecrust. Microwave on High 8 to 9 minutes or until set. Let stand until cool.

Cherry Cake Crisp

Makes 6 servings

- 2 tablespoons sugar
- 4 teaspoons cornstarch
- 1 teaspoon grated orange peel
  Dash salt
- 1 can (16 ounces) pie cherries, drained; reserve syrup
- 1 package (9 ounces) white cake mix
- ¼ teaspoon ground nutmeg
- ¼ cup butter *or* margarine
- ⅓ cup chopped nuts
  Vanilla ice cream

In an 8- or 9-inch round microsafe baking dish, combine sugar, cornstarch, orange peel, and salt. Blend in reserved cherry syrup. Microwave on High 2 minutes. Stir in cherries. Microwave on High 1½ minutes or until bubbly, stirring every 30 seconds. Combine cake mix and nutmeg. Cut in butter with a pastry blender or two knives until the particles are the consistency of small peas. Stir in nuts. Sprinkle cake mixture over cherries. Microwave on High about 14 minutes, turning dish ¼ turn every 2 minutes. Topping will appear slightly moist when the cake is done. Serve warm with ice cream.

Chocolate Pistachio Fudge

Makes about 36 pieces

- 1 pound powdered sugar
- ⅔ cup unsweetened cocoa
- ¼ teaspoon salt
- ¼ cup milk
- 2 teaspoons vanilla
- ¼ teaspoon pistachio flavoring, optional
- ½ cup butter *or* margarine, cut in pieces
- ½ cup chopped pistachio nuts

Butter an 8-inch square baking pan. In a large microsafe bowl, combine powdered sugar, cocoa, and salt. Blend in milk and vanilla. Dot top with butter. Microwave on High for 2 minutes. Remove from oven; beat until smooth. Stir in pistachios. Spread in the prepared pan. Chill about 1 hour or until firm. Cut into pieces.

Date Torte

Makes 12 servings

½ pound pitted dates, cut in pieces
¾ cup water
3 tablespoons butter
1 teaspoon baking soda
2 eggs
1 cup sugar
1 cup sifted flour, divided
1 cup chopped nuts
1 cup whipping cream, whipped
1 can (16 ounces) chocolate-flavored syrup

Grease an 11 x 7-inch microsafe baking pan. In a large microsafe bowl, combine dates, water, and butter. Microwave on High 6 to 8 minutes, stirring every 2 minutes. Let stand 2 minutes. Stir in baking soda. Let stand until cool. In a small bowl, combine eggs, sugar, and ½ cup flour; blend well. Stir remaining ½ cup flour and nuts into the date mixture. Add egg mixture to date mixture; blend well. Pour into the prepared pan. Microwave on High for 8 to 10 minutes, rotating the bowl ¼ turn every 2 minutes. Let stand until cool. Top with whipped cream and chocolate syrup.

Party Pink Pears

Makes 6 servings

6 ripe firm Comice *or* Bartlett pears
6 whole cloves
1 cup sugar
½ cup sweet vermouth
¼ cup water
1 tablespoon lemon juice
½ teaspoon red food coloring
    Sweetened whipped cream

Peel pears, leaving stems intact. Insert 1 clove into each pear. In a 1½-quart microsafe casserole, combine the next 5 ingredients; blend well. Place pears on their sides in casserole. Cover and microwave on High for 6 minutes. Baste pears with syrup. Turn pears over. Cover and microwave on High 6 minutes or until tender. Place pears in individual serving dishes. Spoon syrup over pears. Serve topped with whipped cream.

Amaretto Cake

Makes 12 to 16 servings

½ cup ground pecans
1 package (18.5 ounces) white cake mix
1 box (3 ounces) instant vanilla pudding mix
1 can (12 ounces) almond filling
4 eggs
½ cup vegetable oil
½ cup Amaretto
½ cup water
    Amaretto Glaze (recipe follows)
    Sweetened whipped cream

Lightly grease a microsafe 12-inch fluted tube pan. Sprinkle ground pecans evenly over the bottom. In a large bowl, combine cake mix, pudding mix, and almond filling; blend well. Add eggs, oil, Amaretto, and water. Beat for 4 minutes. Pour into the prepared pan. Microwave on High 11 minutes, rotating the pan ¼ turn every 2 minutes. Cool in the pan 10 minutes. Pour Amaretto Glaze over the cake. Let stand until the glaze is absorbed. Turn out onto a serving plate. Serve with whipped cream.

Amaretto Glaze

½ cup margarine
½ cup sugar
¼ cup Amaretto
¼ cup water

In a 4-cup measure melt margarine on High for 1 minute. Add sugar, Amaretto, and water. Bring to a boil on High; boil for 2 minutes, stirring once.

Easy Almond Bark

Makes about 1½ pounds

1 cup whole blanched almonds
1 teaspoon butter *or* margarine
1 pound white chocolate
2 teaspoons almond extract

Line a large baking sheet with waxed paper. In a microsafe pie plate, combine almonds and butter. Microwave on High 4 minutes or until almonds are golden, stirring every 1½ minutes; set aside. In a large microsafe bowl, place chocolate. Microwave on High 2½ minutes or until softened. Stir in almond extract. Pour onto prepared baking sheet. Spread to about ¼-inch thickness. Let stand until cool. Break into pieces.

Foreign Specialties

Linzertorte

Makes 10 servings

- 1½ cups butter
- 1 cup powdered sugar
- 1 egg
- 1½ cups ground hazelnuts
- Pinch salt
- ½ teaspoon ground cinnamon
- 2¾ cups sifted flour
- 2 cups raspberry jam, divided
- 2 teaspoons lemon juice

In a large bowl, cream butter and sugar until light and fluffy. Blend in the egg. In a separate bowl, combine hazelnuts, salt, and cinnamon. Add the flour alternately with the hazelnut mixture to the creamed mixture; blend well. Chill the dough until firm. Press ⅔ of the dough onto the bottom and 1 inch up the side of a 9-inch springform pan. Roll egg-sized balls of the remaining dough into strips about 8 inches long and ½ inch in diameter. Place on a baking sheet and chill until firm. Mix 1½ cups jam and lemon juice; spread over the dough. With the chilled strips of dough, weave a lattice crust. Bake at 375° F. for 40 minutes. Cool in a pan on a wire rack. Spoon remaining jam into the openings of the lattice crust.

Baklava

Makes about 60 pieces

- 2 cups finely chopped walnuts
- 2 tablespoons sugar
- ½ teaspoon ground cinnamon
- ⅛ teaspoon ground cloves
- ⅛ teaspoon ground allspice
- 1 pound phyllo dough
- 1 pound butter, melted
- Sugar and Honey Syrup (recipe follows)

In a small bowl, mix nuts, sugar, and spices; set aside. Preheat oven to 350° F. Place 1 sheet of phyllo dough on a flat surface. Brush generously with melted butter. Add another sheet of phyllo; brush with butter. Repeat with 3 more sheets of phyllo. Sprinkle nut mixture thinly over half of dough. Roll up, jelly-roll fashion. Place, cut side down, on a large baking sheet. Brush with butter. Chill about 15 minutes. Score dough diagonally with a sharp knife, making cuts about 1 inch apart and cutting no more than ⅛ inch into dough. Repeat for remaining phyllo dough and nut mixture. Bake 2 rolls at a time for 45 minutes or until golden. Cool on baking sheet. Pour hot Sugar and Honey Syrup over each roll. Let the rolls stand several hours or overnight to absorb the syrup. Cut into pieces and serve.

Sugar and Honey Syrup

- 2 cups sugar
- 1 cup water
- 3 tablespoons honey
- 1 stick cinnamon
- 2 whole cloves
- 2 tablespoons brandy, optional
- 1 teaspoon lemon juice

In a small saucepan, combine all ingredients except brandy and lemon juice. Bring to boiling; simmer gently 8 minutes. Stir in lemon juice; simmer 2 minutes. Stir in brandy; simmer 1 minute. Strain syrup to remove spices.

Sandbakkels

Makes about 5 dozen

- 1 cup butter
- ½ cup firmly packed brown sugar
- ½ cup powdered sugar
- 1 egg
- 1 tablespoon vanilla
- 3 cups flour

Preheat oven to 400° F. In a mixing bowl, cream butter and brown sugar until light and fluffy. Add powdered sugar; blend well. Blend in the egg and vanilla. Gradually stir in flour to make a fairly stiff dough. Press pieces of the dough into sandbakkel or tart tins. Bake for 10 minutes. Cool in tins for 1 or 2 minutes before carefully turning out.

Chinese Honeyed Rice Cakes

Makes 4 to 6 servings

    1 cup long-grain rice
1½ cups water
    Vegetable oil
    2 tablespoons sesame seed
    2 tablespoons chopped peanuts
    3 tablespoons honey

In a saucepan, combine rice and water; bring to a boil. Cover and simmer for 25 to 30 minutes or until rice is tender. Preheat oven to 150° F. Spread rice on a large baking sheet. Bake until completely dried, about 6 hours, stirring occasionally. Break the rice into large cakes. Heat oil for deep frying to 400° F. Deep-fry the rice cakes until puffed; drain on paper towels. Sprinkle sesame seed and peanuts over rice cakes. In a small saucepan, warm honey over low heat. Drizzle honey over rice cakes; stir gently. Let the cakes stand until set. Cut or break into small pieces.

French Yule Log

Makes 6 servings

    5 large eggs
    1 egg yolk
¾ cup sugar
½ teaspoon vanilla
¾ cup flour
    3 tablespoons butter, melted
    Custard Cream Filling (recipe follows)
    Chocolate Buttercream Icing (recipe follows)
    Candied cherries, optional

Lightly butter a 16 x 12-inch baking pan. Line pan with waxed paper. Butter and flour the waxed paper; set aside. Preheat oven to 325° F. In a large bowl, combine eggs, egg yolk, sugar, and vanilla. Place the bowl in a pan of hot water. With an electric mixer, beat the egg mixture at high speed for 5 to 6 minutes. Remove bowl from hot water. Sift flour over egg mixture and gently fold it in with a rubber spatula. Fold in the melted butter. Spread the batter evenly in the prepared pan. Bake for 12 minutes or until golden. After cake has cooled in the pan for 5 minutes, turn out of pan and carefully peel off the waxed paper. Cover the cake loosely with waxed paper. Let cool for about 5 minutes to let the steam escape and the dough firm up. Place the cake between 2 sheets of waxed paper. Roll up lengthwise. Refrigerate until ready to use. Prepare Custard Cream Filling and Chocolate Buttercream Icing. Unroll the cake

and spread with Custard Filling. Roll up the cake lengthwise. Cut a 2-inch slice from each end of the cake. Place the cake on a serving platter. Place the 2-inch slices on opposite sides of cake to form "stumps." Use a small amount of Chocolate Buttercream Icing to hold them in place. Spread chocolate buttercream over the cake, but do not frost the cut edges. Spread the reserved ¼ cup plain buttercream on the four cut edges. Pull a fork the length of the cake to simulate bark. Fill a pastry bag with reserved ¼ cup chocolate buttercream. Pipe rings onto ends of "log" and "stumps" to simulate wood. Garnish with candied cherries and holly leaves, if desired.

Custard Cream Filling

    3 egg yolks
⅓ cup sugar
½ teaspoon vanilla
¼ cup flour
    1 cup boiling milk
½ cup whipping cream

In a mixing bowl, combine egg yolks, sugar, and vanilla. Beat until thickened and light-colored. Blend in the flour. Gradually add milk; stir with a wire whisk until well blended. Transfer to a saucepan. Cook over medium heat, stirring constantly until mixture boils. Simmer, stirring constantly, 2 to 3 minutes. Remove from heat. Cover and let stand until cool. In a small mixing bowl, beat whipping cream until stiff peaks form. Fold whipped cream into custard.

Chocolate Buttercream Icing

⅓ cup sugar
¼ cup water
    3 egg yolks
½ pound butter, softened
    3 squares (1 ounce each) semisweet baking chocolate, melted
    2 squares (1 ounce each) unsweetened baking chocolate, melted

In a small saucepan, combine sugar and water. Bring to a boil; boil to 236° F. on a candy thermometer. Remove from heat. In a small bowl, beat the eggs until well blended. Gradually beat in the hot sugar syrup for 5 minutes or until thickened and light-colored. Add butter, a little at a time, beating on low speed until smooth. Reserve ¼ cup of the buttercream. Beat the melted chocolate into the remaining portion until smooth. Set aside ¼ cup chocolate buttercream.

Index